Understanding Our World

Tom Sotis

Understanding Our World

ISBN # 978-1-300-96105-5

Imprint: Lulu.com

To my good friend

David Hayes

Contents

Introduction: Why Understanding the World Matters

In the 21st century, the world has become more interconnected and complex than at any other point in history. As technology shrinks geographical barriers, political events on one side of the globe can ripple across to the other in an instant, and economic shifts in one region can send shockwaves throughout the global marketplace. People across continents are now linked by intricate networks of trade, communication, and culture. This has made it essential to not only be aware of what is happening in the world but also to understand the forces shaping our lives and the environment we live in. In a world characterized by rapid change, unpredictability, and complexity, knowledge and awareness are no longer luxuries — they are necessities.

Understanding the world around us goes far beyond simply staying informed about current events or acquiring technical knowledge. It requires a deep awareness of the historical, cultural, scientific, and political forces that shape societies and drive human behavior. It involves questioning assumptions, recognizing biases, and approaching problems with a critical mindset. Understanding the world matters because it empowers individuals to navigate life's challenges with greater clarity and purpose. It allows people to make informed decisions, connect more meaningfully with others, and contribute positively to society. This book aims to provide readers with a framework for thinking critically and understanding the complexities of the world in which we live.

The Importance of Knowledge and Awareness in Today's Global Society

In today's world, knowledge is more accessible than ever before. The internet has democratized information, giving people the ability to learn about any topic at the click of a button. However, the sheer volume of information available can also be overwhelming. In this environment, it is easy to become passive consumers of information, scrolling through endless streams of headlines, social media posts, and videos without fully engaging with the content or critically assessing its validity. This can lead to a superficial understanding of important issues or, worse, falling prey to misinformation and conspiracy theories.

In contrast, true knowledge involves not only accessing information but also analyzing and synthesizing it in a meaningful way. It requires discernment, reflection, and a commitment to lifelong learning. Knowledge is not static; it is a dynamic process that evolves as we encounter new ideas, experiences, and perspectives. In a global society where cultures, economies, and political systems are interwoven, the ability to engage with different forms of knowledge is critical. Whether it is understanding the cultural context behind international conflicts or grasping the economic principles driving global markets, informed individuals are better equipped to make sense of the world around them and engage with it effectively.

Awareness, meanwhile, goes beyond intellectual understanding to encompass an emotional and ethical dimension. It involves recognizing the interconnectedness of human life and being attuned to the ways in which our actions, decisions, and values affect others. In a globalized world, where the effects of climate change, pandemics, and technological advancements are felt across borders, cultivating awareness is crucial for fostering a sense of global citizenship. When individuals are aware of the broader implications of their actions, they are more likely to act in ways that promote social justice, environmental sustainability, and collective well-being.

How the World is Interconnected Through Culture, Politics, Science, and History

To truly understand the world, one must recognize the many ways in which it is interconnected. At first glance, the world may seem fragmented by national borders, cultural differences, and political ideologies. But beneath these surface-level divisions lies a complex web of interdependence that connects people across continents and cultures. This interdependence can be seen in many areas of life, including culture, politics, science, and history.

Culture and Globalization

Culture is one of the most powerful forces that connect people and shape their understanding of the world. It influences everything from language, religion, and art to social norms, values, and traditions. While cultures vary across the globe, the process of globalization has brought different cultures into closer contact than ever before. Through trade, travel, and the media, cultural ideas and practices are exchanged, blended, and adapted in new and exciting ways. For example, people in Europe might enjoy sushi, a traditional Japanese dish, while people in Asia listen to hip-hop, a music genre that originated in the United States.

At the same time, globalization also presents challenges. The rapid spread of Western cultural products, such as fast food, movies, and fashion, has raised concerns about cultural homogenization, where local cultures risk being overshadowed by global trends. Understanding the global flow of culture is essential for appreciating both the richness of diversity and the potential for cultural erosion in a globalized world.

Politics and International Relations

Politics is another critical area where the world's interconnections are clearly visible. National governments no longer operate in isolation; they are part of a global political system where decisions made in one country can have far-reaching consequences. International organizations, such as the United Nations, the World Trade Organization, and the European Union, play an increasingly important role in shaping global policies on issues ranging from human rights to climate change. Political alliances, treaties, and trade agreements bind countries together in ways that require cooperation and diplomacy.

In addition to formal political structures, global politics is shaped by non-state actors, such as multinational corporations, non-governmental organizations (NGOs), and even social movements. The power dynamics between these actors can influence everything from global security to economic stability. For instance, the influence of multinational corporations in shaping trade policies, labor practices, and environmental regulations can have profound effects on local communities and ecosystems. Understanding these political dynamics is crucial for anyone seeking to grasp how power is distributed and exercised on a global scale.

Science and Technological Advancements

Science and technology have been key drivers of global interconnectedness. From the development of the steam engine in the Industrial Revolution to the advent of the internet in the Information Age, scientific breakthroughs have transformed the way people live, work, and communicate. Advances in medicine, transportation, and energy have not only improved the quality of life for many but have also brought the world closer together. The ability to travel across continents in a matter of hours or to communicate with someone on the other side of the world in real-time has fundamentally changed the way people interact and share knowledge.

However, scientific advancements also come with new ethical and existential challenges. The development of nuclear weapons, for example, raised profound questions about the use of science for destructive purposes. More recently, debates over the ethics of artificial intelligence, genetic engineering, and data privacy highlight the complexities of navigating a world where technological innovation often outpaces regulation and ethical guidelines. In this context, understanding science is not just about knowing how things work — it's about understanding the broader implications of scientific progress for society and the environment.

History's Influence on the Present

Finally, history provides a lens through which we can understand the interconnectedness of the world. History is not a series of isolated events but a continuous process in which past actions shape present realities. The legacies of colonialism, slavery, and imperialism, for example, continue to influence global power dynamics, economic inequalities, and racial tensions. Understanding the historical roots of contemporary issues is essential for making sense of current events and for working toward solutions that address deep-seated injustices.

Moreover, history teaches us that societies are constantly evolving, influenced by the rise and fall of empires, the spread of ideas, and the resilience of cultures. Historical knowledge allows us to see patterns, learn from mistakes, and appreciate the complexity of human development. In a world where historical amnesia can lead to repeated mistakes, fostering a deep understanding of history is critical for informed decision-making and responsible citizenship.

The Book's Goal: A Framework for Thinking Critically

The primary goal of this book is to provide readers with a framework for thinking critically and understanding the complexities of the world in which we live. Critical thinking is more than just a cognitive skill; it is a way of approaching the world with curiosity, openness, and a willingness to question assumptions. In a world where information is abundant but often misleading, the ability to think critically is invaluable.

This book will explore various aspects of human life — including culture, politics, science, history, economics, and psychology — to help readers develop a more nuanced and comprehensive understanding of the world. Each chapter will delve into key concepts and ideas that are essential for making sense of the world's complexities. By the end of the book, readers will be equipped with the tools they need to engage with the world in a more thoughtful and informed way.

Conclusion

Understanding the world is not an easy task, but it is an essential one. In a global society marked by interdependence, rapid change, and uncertainty, knowledge and awareness are the keys to navigating the challenges of the modern world. By understanding the cultural, political, scientific, and historical forces that shape our lives, we can make better decisions, engage more meaningfully with others, and contribute to a more just and sustainable world. This book is an invitation to embark on a journey of discovery, reflection, and critical thinking — a journey that will ultimately lead to a deeper understanding of the world we all share.

Chapter 1: The Power of Perspective

Understanding Different Worldviews and Their Impact on How People See Reality

Imagine two people standing on opposite sides of a mountain. One side is lush and green, filled with trees and vegetation, while the other is arid and rocky, a stark desert landscape. When each person describes the mountain, they provide entirely different accounts. To the one on the green side, the mountain represents life, fertility, and abundance. To the other, it signifies harshness, survival, and struggle. Both descriptions are valid, yet they are limited by the perspective of each individual.

This simple metaphor illustrates a profound truth about human experience: our perspective shapes our reality. The way we see the world is influenced by our surroundings, our experiences, and the particular "lens" through which we view life. This lens is shaped by countless factors, including our culture, religion, upbringing, education, personal experiences, and even the media we consume. These various influences combine to form what is often referred to as a "worldview"—a comprehensive framework through which we interpret the world and make sense of our place in it.

A worldview is more than just a set of beliefs or opinions; it is the foundation of how we perceive reality itself. It affects how we interpret events, how we make decisions, and how we relate to others. For example, someone with a scientific worldview may prioritize evidence and data when forming opinions about the world, while someone with a more spiritual or religious worldview may see the hand of a higher power in everyday occurrences. Similarly, individuals raised in individualistic cultures might view personal freedom and autonomy as paramount, while those from collectivist cultures may prioritize community and social harmony.

These worldviews are not fixed or immutable; they can evolve over time as people gain new experiences, encounter new ideas, or reflect on their beliefs. However, worldviews can also be deeply ingrained, sometimes to the point where people are unaware of how their own perspective shapes their interpretation of reality. This is why it is so important to cultivate an awareness of different worldviews and the impact they have on our understanding of the world. By recognizing the diversity of perspectives that exist, we can develop a more nuanced and empathetic approach to understanding others—and ourselves.

The Subjectivity of Reality

One of the most important insights we can gain from examining different worldviews is the recognition that reality is not as objective or universal as we might like to believe. What we perceive as "truth" is often colored by our individual perspective. This doesn't mean that there are no objective facts—science, for example, relies on empirical evidence to establish certain truths about the physical world. However, when it comes to interpreting social, political, and cultural realities, our perspectives can vary widely.

Consider, for instance, the concept of success. In some cultures, success is measured by financial wealth, career achievements, or material possessions. In others, success may be defined by one's contributions to the community, the well-being of one's family, or spiritual fulfillment. Both definitions of success are valid, but they are shaped by the cultural context in which they are situated.

Another example is the way people view conflict or war. In some societies, war is seen as a necessary means of defending freedom or achieving justice. In others, it is regarded as a last resort, an avoidable tragedy that disrupts lives and creates suffering. The same historical event can be interpreted very differently depending on who is telling the story and from which perspective. For example, colonialism is often portrayed as a "civilizing mission" by the colonizers, but from the perspective of the colonized, it is remembered as a period of oppression and exploitation.

These examples highlight the power of perspective in shaping our understanding of the world. What we perceive as "normal," "right," or "true" is often a reflection of our own worldview. By acknowledging the subjectivity of our perspective, we can begin to question assumptions, challenge biases, and open ourselves up to alternative ways of seeing the world.

How Culture, Upbringing, and Personal Experiences Shape One's Understanding of the World

Our worldview is not something we are born with—it is something we develop over time, shaped by a myriad of influences. Among the most significant of these influences are culture, upbringing, and personal experiences. Each of these factors plays a crucial role in determining how we see the world, how we interpret events, and how we interact with others.

Culture: The Collective Lens

Culture can be understood as the shared values, beliefs, practices, and traditions that bind a group of people together. It encompasses everything from language and religion to art, music, food, and social norms. Culture is often described as a "collective lens" through which people perceive the world, and it has a profound impact on shaping one's worldview.

For example, in many Western cultures, there is a strong emphasis on individualism—the idea that personal autonomy and self-expression are fundamental to human fulfillment. This worldview influences everything from parenting styles to political ideologies, with a focus on personal rights and freedoms. In contrast, many Asian cultures emphasize collectivism, which prioritizes the needs and well-being of the group—whether that group is the family, the community, or the nation—over individual desires. In collectivist societies, harmony, cooperation, and social responsibility are often valued more highly than individual achievement or self-expression.

These cultural differences are not simply abstract concepts; they shape the way people approach everyday life. For example, in individualistic cultures, people might place a high value on personal success and self-reliance, while in collectivist cultures, people may prioritize their role within the family or community. These differing values can influence everything from career choices and relationships to political beliefs and social attitudes.

Culture also shapes how people interpret events and behaviors. A gesture that is considered polite in one culture might be seen as rude or inappropriate in another. For example, in some Middle Eastern cultures, it is customary to greet people with a kiss on the cheek, while in many Western cultures, a firm handshake is the norm. Similarly, direct eye contact is often interpreted as a sign of confidence and honesty in Western cultures, while in some Asian cultures, it can be seen as disrespectful or confrontational.

The key takeaway is that culture profoundly shapes our understanding of the world, and it influences the way we think, feel, and behave. By recognizing the role that culture plays in shaping our worldview, we can develop a greater appreciation for cultural diversity and become more open to perspectives that differ from our own.

Upbringing: The Foundation of Worldview

While culture provides the broader context in which we develop our worldview, upbringing plays a more personal and immediate role in shaping our perspective. From a young age, our families, caregivers, and communities instill in us certain values, beliefs, and expectations. These early influences form the foundation of our worldview, and they often continue to shape our understanding of the world well into adulthood.

For example, children raised in religious households may grow up with a strong sense of faith and spirituality, which can shape their understanding of morality, ethics, and the meaning of life. In contrast, children raised in secular households may develop a more humanistic or scientific approach to these same questions. Similarly, children raised in politically active families may develop a strong sense of civic duty and engagement, while those raised in apolitical households may be less interested in politics or social issues.

The environment in which we are raised also plays a significant role in shaping our worldview. Children who grow up in urban areas may be exposed to a diverse range of cultures, languages, and perspectives, which can foster open-mindedness and adaptability. In contrast, children raised in more homogenous or insular communities may have fewer opportunities to encounter different worldviews, which can result in a more limited or parochial perspective.

Our upbringing also influences how we respond to challenges and adversity. Children who are raised in supportive, nurturing environments may develop a strong sense of resilience and self-confidence, while those who experience trauma, neglect, or instability may struggle with feelings of insecurity or mistrust. These early experiences can shape our understanding of the world as either a safe and predictable place or as a dangerous and uncertain one.

It is important to note that while upbringing plays a significant role in shaping our worldview, it is not deterministic. People can and do change their perspectives as they grow older, encounter new experiences, and reflect on their beliefs. However, the values and beliefs instilled during childhood often form the foundation upon which future experiences are built.

Personal Experiences: Shaping Perception Through Life

While culture and upbringing provide the initial framework for our worldview, personal experiences are what give it depth and texture. As we move through life, we encounter a wide range of experiences—both positive and negative—that shape our understanding of the world. These experiences can include everything from travel and education to relationships, work, and personal challenges.

For example, someone who has traveled extensively may develop a more cosmopolitan and open-minded perspective, having been exposed to different cultures, languages, and ways of life. In contrast, someone who has spent their entire life in one place may have a more limited or parochial perspective. Similarly, someone who has faced significant personal challenges—such as illness, loss, or discrimination—may develop a greater sense of empathy and resilience, while someone who has lived a more sheltered or privileged life may have less experience with adversity.

Our personal experiences also shape how we interpret events and behaviors. For example, someone who has experienced discrimination may be more attuned to issues of social justice and inequality, while someone who has not faced such challenges may be less aware of these issues. Similarly, someone who has worked in a particular industry or profession may have a deeper understanding of the complexities and nuances of that field, while someone with no experience in that area may have a more superficial or simplistic understanding.

Personal experiences can also lead to significant shifts in worldview. For example, someone who grows up in a conservative household may adopt more liberal views after attending college or traveling abroad. Similarly, someone who has a near-death experience may develop a newfound appreciation for life and a deeper sense of spirituality. These experiences can challenge our assumptions, broaden our horizons, and ultimately lead to a more complex and nuanced understanding of the world.

The Benefits of Developing a Global Mindset

In an increasingly interconnected and globalized world, developing a global mindset is more important than ever. A global mindset refers to the ability to understand, appreciate, and navigate different cultures, perspectives, and worldviews. It involves being open to new ideas, being willing to question assumptions, and being able to see the world from multiple perspectives.

One of the key benefits of developing a global mindset is that it fosters greater empathy and understanding. When we are able to see the world through the eyes of others, we are better able to understand their experiences, values, and motivations. This, in turn, can lead to more meaningful and respectful interactions, both on a personal and a global level.

A global mindset also promotes adaptability and resilience. In a world that is constantly changing, being able to navigate different cultural and social contexts is an invaluable skill. People with a global mindset are more likely to embrace change, seek out new experiences, and remain open to new ideas. This adaptability is particularly important in the workplace, where globalization and technological advancements are reshaping industries and creating new challenges and opportunities.

Moreover, developing a global mindset can lead to more informed decision-making. When we are able to consider multiple perspectives, we are less likely to fall into the trap of "groupthink" or to make decisions based on limited or biased information. A global mindset encourages critical thinking, creativity, and problem-solving, all of which are essential for navigating the complexities of the modern world.

Finally, a global mindset fosters a sense of global citizenship. In a world where issues like climate change, pandemics, and economic inequality transcend national borders, it is more important than ever to think and act in ways that promote the common good. A global mindset encourages people to see themselves as part of a larger, interconnected world and to take responsibility for the impact of their actions on others.

Conclusion

Perspective is one of the most powerful tools we have for understanding the world. Our worldview shapes how we see reality, how we interpret events, and how we interact with others. By recognizing the role that culture, upbringing, and personal experiences play in shaping our perspective, we can develop a greater awareness of the diversity of worldviews that exist. Moreover, by cultivating a global mindset, we can foster greater empathy, adaptability, and informed decision-making, all of which are essential for navigating the complexities of the modern world.

Understanding the power of perspective is the first step toward developing a more nuanced and comprehensive understanding of the world. In the chapters that follow, we will explore other key aspects of human life, culture, science, and history that contribute to a deeper understanding of the world we live in. By the end of this journey, you will be better equipped to think critically, challenge assumptions, and engage with the world in a more thoughtful and informed way.

Chapter 2: History as a Guide

History is not just a record of past events; it is the foundation upon which the present stands and the lens through which we can better understand the future. As the famous saying goes, "Those who cannot remember the past are condemned to repeat it." In today's rapidly changing world, the relevance of history has never been more vital. The study of history helps us contextualize modern challenges, understand the forces that shape our societies, and learn from the triumphs and mistakes of those who came before us.

In this chapter, we will explore why history is crucial to understanding the present, examine key historical events that shaped modern civilization, and discuss how learning from history's lessons can help us navigate the future with wisdom and foresight.

Why History is Crucial to Understanding the Present

To understand the significance of history, we must first recognize its pervasive influence on every aspect of life today. Whether we are aware of it or not, our political systems, cultural norms, economic structures, and even the technology we use are the products of centuries of historical development. History shapes the stories we tell ourselves about who we are, where we come from, and what our societies stand for.

The Continuity Between Past and Present

The past is never truly gone. It lives on in our institutions, in our customs, and in the collective memory of societies. The laws we follow, the languages we speak, and the borders that define our countries are all products of historical processes.

Events such as wars, revolutions, and movements for independence have left an indelible mark on the way nations function and how people see themselves in relation to the world.

Take, for example, the modern political landscape. The democratic systems that exist today in many parts of the world are the result of long struggles for representation and human rights. In the Western world, the roots of democracy can be traced back to ancient Greece, but its modern form owes much to the Enlightenment ideals of the 18th century and the revolutions that followed. The American Revolution (1776), the French Revolution (1789), and the decolonization movements of the 20th century all played pivotal roles in shaping today's global political order.

However, history's influence is not confined to politics. The economic inequalities, cultural differences, and social issues we see today are often direct consequences of historical events. Colonialism, for instance, reshaped the world's political and economic map. The exploitation of resources and people during the colonial period continues to have ripple effects in the economic disparities between the Global North and Global South. To truly understand the modern world's wealth gaps, one must understand the historical processes of imperialism, slavery, and exploitation that created and maintained them.

By recognizing this continuity between past and present, we gain a more nuanced understanding of today's challenges. Without the context that history provides, we are left with an incomplete picture, unable to grasp the complexities of current events. Whether we are analyzing social movements, economic policies, or international relations, a historical perspective is essential for meaningful analysis.

History's Role in Identity Formation

History also plays a crucial role in shaping individual and collective identities. Nations, communities, and even individuals draw on historical narratives to define themselves. This process of identity formation is complex and often involves the selective remembering and forgetting of historical events. As a result, different groups may interpret the same historical events in vastly different ways.

For example, the American Civil War is often viewed differently by various communities within the United States. For many, it is a war fought over the moral issue of slavery and the preservation of the Union. For others, particularly in the Southern states, the war may be remembered as a fight for states' rights and regional autonomy. These differing interpretations continue to influence how Americans see themselves and their nation's history.

The same can be said on a global scale. Different nations remember and commemorate historical events in ways that reflect their national values and political agendas. The World Wars, for example, are remembered in starkly different terms depending on where one stands. For Europeans, they represent devastation and the collapse of old empires, but for Americans, they are often framed as heroic struggles that cemented the United States as a world power. In Japan, the memory of World War II is fraught with debates over accountability and victimhood, particularly in relation to the atomic bombings of Hiroshima and Nagasaki.

These differing historical memories can be a source of tension and conflict, but they also demonstrate the power of history in shaping identity. By understanding how historical narratives are constructed and used, we can better appreciate the complexities of modern identities and the often competing versions of history that shape contemporary discourse.

The Importance of Contextualizing Modern Issues

In today's world, the speed of change can often make it seem as though the past is irrelevant. However, understanding the historical context behind modern issues is crucial for addressing them effectively. For example, the ongoing debates about immigration, race relations, and economic inequality cannot be fully understood without examining the historical roots of these issues.

Take immigration as an example. Immigration is often portrayed as a contemporary issue, but migration has been a constant throughout human history. Whether it was the mass movements of people during the Roman Empire, the forced migration of Africans during the transatlantic slave trade, or the European emigration to the Americas in the 19th and 20th centuries, migration has long shaped the world's demographic and cultural landscape. Today's debates about immigration are often a continuation of these historical patterns, with new layers of complexity added by globalization, technology, and changing political dynamics.

Similarly, race relations in many parts of the world are deeply rooted in historical processes such as colonization, slavery, and segregation. The legacy of these injustices continues to affect marginalized communities today. Understanding this history is essential for addressing systemic inequalities and working toward more just and equitable societies.

In short, history is not a distant or irrelevant subject—it is a vital tool for understanding the present. By looking to the past, we can gain valuable insights into the forces that shape our world and the challenges we face today.

Key Historical Events that Shaped Modern Civilization

Throughout history, certain events have had a profound and lasting impact on the development of human civilization. These events did not occur in isolation; they were the result of complex historical processes involving political, economic, social, and cultural factors. In this section, we will explore some of the most significant historical events that have shaped modern civilization, focusing on how they continue to influence the world today.

The Agricultural Revolution (c. 10,000 BCE)

One of the most transformative events in human history was the **Agricultural Revolution**, which began around 10,000 BCE. Before this period, human societies were primarily hunter-gatherers, relying on foraging and hunting for survival. The development of agriculture marked a radical shift in how humans interacted with the environment and with each other.

The ability to cultivate crops and domesticate animals allowed for the growth of stable, sedentary communities. This, in turn, led to the rise of complex societies, the development of social hierarchies, and the eventual emergence of cities and states. The Agricultural Revolution laid the groundwork for all subsequent human civilizations, making possible advancements in technology, art, politics, and economics.

The effects of the Agricultural Revolution continue to resonate today. Our modern food systems, economies, and social structures are all built upon the foundation laid by early agricultural societies. The shift to agriculture also introduced new challenges, such as population growth, resource depletion, and social inequality—issues that still confront us today.

The Rise and Fall of the Roman Empire (27 BCE – 476 CE)

The **Roman Empire** was one of the most powerful and influential civilizations in human history. At its height, the empire stretched across much of Europe, North Africa, and the Middle East, encompassing diverse cultures and peoples. The Roman Empire left a lasting legacy in many areas, including law, governance, architecture, and language.

Roman law, for example, laid the foundation for many modern legal systems, particularly in Europe and Latin America. Concepts such as property rights, contracts, and citizenship, which were codified in Roman law, continue to influence legal frameworks around the world. Additionally, Roman engineering feats, such as aqueducts, roads, and public buildings, set a standard for urban development that continues to inspire architects and planners today.

However, the fall of the Roman Empire in 476 CE marked the beginning of a period of political fragmentation and instability in Europe, known as the Middle Ages. The decline of centralized authority led to the rise of feudalism, a system in which local lords held power and allegiance was based on personal relationships rather than a unified state. Despite the fall of the empire, Roman culture and institutions continued to influence European society through the Christian Church and the preservation of Roman texts.

The Roman Empire's legacy is still evident today in the political and cultural structures of Western civilization. The concept of republicanism, for example, which originated in the Roman Republic, has inspired modern democratic movements, while Latin, the language of the Romans, remains the root of many European languages.

The Age of Exploration (15th – 17th Century)

The **Age of Exploration** marked a turning point in world history. Beginning in the 15th century, European explorers set out to discover new trade routes and territories, driven by a desire for wealth, power, and the spread of Christianity. Figures like Christopher Columbus, Vasco da Gama, and Ferdinand Magellan are often remembered as pioneers of this era, though their voyages also had devastating consequences for indigenous populations.

The Age of Exploration led to the establishment of European colonies in the Americas, Africa, and Asia, setting the stage for centuries of global trade, cultural exchange, and exploitation. European powers grew wealthy from the resources they extracted from their colonies, while indigenous peoples were often subjected to violence, enslavement, and displacement. The transatlantic slave trade, in particular, was a direct result of European colonization and had a profound impact on the development of the Americas and the global economy.

The legacy of the Age of Exploration continues to shape the world today. Modern global trade networks, economic systems, and cultural exchanges are all products of the colonial period. At the same time, the social and economic inequalities that arose during this era continue to affect marginalized communities, particularly in the Global South.

The Industrial Revolution (18th – 19th Century)

The **Industrial Revolution** was a period of profound technological and economic change that began in Britain in the late 18th century and spread to other parts of Europe and North America. It marked a shift from agrarian economies, in which goods were produced by hand, to industrial economies, in which goods were produced by machines in factories.

The Industrial Revolution brought about unprecedented levels of productivity and wealth, but it also introduced new social and environmental challenges. The rise of factories led to the growth of cities, as people moved from rural areas to urban centers in search of work. This urbanization brought with it overcrowding, poor working conditions, and the exploitation of labor, particularly child labor. At the same time, industrialization had a significant environmental impact, contributing to deforestation, pollution, and the depletion of natural resources.

Despite these challenges, the Industrial Revolution transformed human society in ways that continue to shape the modern world. The technological innovations of this period, such as the steam engine, the spinning jenny, and the telegraph, laid the foundation for the modern industrial economy. Today's global economy, characterized by mass production, international trade, and technological innovation, owes much to the Industrial Revolution.

The World Wars (20th Century)

The **World Wars** of the 20th century were among the most devastating events in human history. World War I (1914–1918) and World War II (1939–1945) reshaped the political, social, and economic landscape of the 20th century and had lasting consequences for the world we live in today.

World War I, often referred to as the "Great War," was a conflict between the world's major powers, triggered by a complex web of alliances, militarism, and nationalism. The war resulted in the collapse of empires, the redrawing of national borders, and the creation of new political ideologies, including communism and fascism. The Treaty of Versailles, which ended the war, imposed harsh penalties on Germany, sowing the seeds for World War II.

World War II, the deadliest conflict in human history, was fought between the Allied Powers (led by the United States, the Soviet Union, and the United Kingdom) and the Axis Powers (led by Nazi Germany, Japan, and Italy). The war resulted in the defeat of fascism and the rise of the United States and the Soviet Union as global superpowers. It also led to the creation of the United Nations, an international organization dedicated to maintaining peace and promoting human rights.

The legacy of the World Wars continues to shape the world today. The geopolitical landscape of the 20th century, including the Cold War and the division of Europe into Eastern and Western blocs, was a direct result of the wars. Additionally, the social and economic upheavals caused by the wars led to significant advances in civil rights, women's rights, and international diplomacy.

Learning from History's Lessons to Better Navigate the Future

History is not only a tool for understanding the present but also a guide for navigating the future. The study of history offers valuable lessons that can help individuals and societies make informed decisions, avoid repeating mistakes, and work toward a more just and equitable world.

The Importance of Critical Thinking

One of the most important lessons we can learn from history is the value of critical thinking. History is not a simple narrative of progress or decline; it is a complex and often contradictory process. By studying history critically, we can develop a more nuanced understanding of the forces that shape human societies.

For example, many people today look back at the Industrial Revolution as a period of technological progress and economic growth. However, a critical examination of this period reveals that industrialization also brought about significant social and environmental challenges, including poverty, exploitation, and environmental degradation. By recognizing these complexities, we can better understand the trade-offs involved in technological and economic development and work toward more sustainable and equitable solutions.

Similarly, studying the causes and consequences of the World Wars can help us develop a more critical perspective on modern geopolitics. The alliances, rivalries, and ideologies that led to the wars were the result of complex historical processes, and understanding these processes can help us avoid repeating the mistakes of the past.

The Importance of Empathy and Understanding

History also teaches us the importance of empathy and understanding. By studying the experiences of people in the past, we can develop a greater appreciation for the diversity of human experience and the challenges faced by different communities.

For example, studying the history of slavery and colonialism can help us develop a deeper understanding of the systemic inequalities that continue to affect marginalized communities today. By recognizing the historical roots of these inequalities, we can work toward more just and equitable solutions.

Similarly, studying the experiences of people during the World Wars can help us develop a greater appreciation for the sacrifices made by previous generations and the importance of peace and diplomacy in resolving conflicts.

The Importance of Adaptability and Resilience

Finally, history teaches us the importance of adaptability and resilience. Human societies have faced numerous challenges throughout history, from natural disasters to pandemics to economic crises. By studying how people in the past have responded to these challenges, we can develop the skills and knowledge needed to navigate the uncertainties of the future.

For example, studying the responses to past pandemics, such as the Black Death or the Spanish flu, can help us better understand the challenges posed by modern pandemics, such as COVID-19. Similarly, studying the responses to economic crises, such as the Great Depression, can help us develop strategies for addressing modern economic challenges.

History is not a static record of the past; it is a dynamic and ever-evolving process. By learning from history's lessons, we can better navigate the future and work toward a more just, equitable, and sustainable world.

Conclusion

History is not just a collection of dates and facts; it is a guide for understanding the present and navigating the future. By studying the past, we can gain valuable insights into the forces that shape our world, the challenges we face, and the opportunities for growth and progress.

From the Agricultural Revolution to the Industrial Revolution, from the rise and fall of empires to the World Wars, history has left an indelible mark on human civilization. By understanding these key historical events, we can better appreciate the complexities of the modern world and work toward a more informed and empathetic approach to the challenges of the future.

As we move forward, let us remember that history is not just a record of what has happened, but a guide for what can happen. By learning from the successes and failures of the past, we can build a more just, equitable, and sustainable future for all.

Chapter 3: The Age of Information

We are living in what is often referred to as the **Information Age**—a period where information has become more accessible, abundant, and transformative than at any other point in human history. As technology continues to evolve, the way we access, distribute, and consume information is constantly changing. This rapid expansion of information networks has revolutionized everything from education and communication to politics and economics, making knowledge and information more critical than ever before.

However, the Information Age comes with its own set of challenges. In a world saturated with information, the ability to distinguish between credible sources and misinformation has become a crucial skill. Information, once a valuable resource that took effort to acquire, is now so abundant that it often overwhelms us, making it difficult to separate truth from falsehood. This chapter explores the evolution of information exchange, the importance of media literacy in an age of misinformation, and the tools necessary for critically assessing sources and information.

The Evolution of Information Exchange: From the Printing Press to the Internet

The way humans exchange information has undergone dramatic transformations over the centuries, and these changes have had profound effects on societies. From the invention of the **printing press** in the 15th century to the rise of the **internet** in the 20th century, each technological leap has expanded the reach of knowledge, democratized information, and reshaped how people communicate.

The Printing Press: A Revolution in Communication

Before the printing press, written information was painstakingly copied by hand. In the Western world, manuscripts were primarily the domain of monks and scholars, kept in religious and academic institutions that were inaccessible to most people. Books were rare and expensive, and literacy rates were low because the vast majority of people had no need for reading in their daily lives.

This all changed in the mid-15th century, when **Johannes Gutenberg** invented the movable type printing press. This innovation allowed for the mass production of books and other printed materials, drastically reducing the cost of books and making them more widely available. The printing press democratized knowledge, enabling the spread of ideas and information on a scale that had never been seen before.

The printing press played a central role in the **Renaissance** and the **Reformation**, two major historical movements that reshaped European society. During the Renaissance, the availability of printed works helped revive interest in classical learning and fostered intellectual exploration. The Reformation, which challenged the authority of the Catholic Church, was made possible in part by the widespread distribution of religious pamphlets and translations of the Bible into vernacular languages. What once took years to transcribe by hand could now be replicated in days or even hours, making ideas more accessible to the masses.

The printing press also laid the groundwork for the development of **modern democracy**. By making books and pamphlets affordable and accessible to a larger audience, it encouraged literacy and the spread of ideas that questioned existing power structures. The dissemination of Enlightenment ideals—such as liberty, equality, and the rights of individuals—was made possible by the printing press, leading to social revolutions and the rise of democratic systems in many parts of the world.

The Telegraph, Radio, and Television: Bridging Distances

In the centuries following Gutenberg's invention, new technologies continued to improve the speed and reach of information exchange. One of the most transformative inventions of the 19th century was the **telegraph**. Invented by **Samuel Morse** in the 1830s, the telegraph made it possible to send messages across vast distances in a matter of minutes. This was a radical improvement over previous methods of communication, such as letters, which could take weeks or even months to travel from one place to another.

The telegraph revolutionized global communication. It allowed governments to coordinate over long distances, facilitated international trade, and played a crucial role in the expansion of railroads and other industries. It also had a profound impact on journalism, giving rise to the **wire service**, which allowed newspapers to report on events from around the world with unprecedented speed and accuracy.

In the 20th century, the development of **radio** and **television** further transformed the media landscape. Radio, first popularized in the 1920s, allowed people to listen to news, music, and entertainment broadcasts from their homes, while television, which became widely available in the 1950s, added a visual element to mass communication. Both radio and television played important roles in shaping public opinion and spreading information, particularly during major global events such as World War II and the Cold War.

These technologies allowed for real-time dissemination of information to mass audiences, bridging the gap between nations and cultures. For the first time in human history, millions of people could share a common experience—whether it was listening to a speech by a political leader, watching the first moon landing, or witnessing the fall of the Berlin Wall—all from their living rooms.

The Internet: The Information Explosion

The most significant leap in the evolution of information exchange came in the late 20th century with the invention of the **internet**. Initially developed as a military project in the 1960s, the internet evolved into a global communication network that connects billions of people across the globe. The internet has radically transformed how information is produced, shared, and consumed.

Unlike previous forms of media, the internet is **decentralized** and **interactive**. Anyone with access to the internet can create and share content, allowing for a diversity of voices and perspectives. Social media platforms, blogs, podcasts, and video-sharing sites have all given individuals and groups the power to bypass traditional gatekeepers, such as publishers or broadcasters, and reach global audiences directly.

This democratization of information has had many positive effects. It has enabled social movements, such as the Arab Spring and #MeToo, to organize and mobilize on a global scale. It has also made education more accessible, with online courses, webinars, and open access resources available to anyone with an internet connection. Moreover, the internet has revolutionized the way we work, shop, and communicate, connecting people and businesses in ways that were once unimaginable.

However, the internet has also introduced new challenges, particularly in terms of information overload and the spread of misinformation. With so much content being produced every second, it can be difficult to distinguish between credible sources and false information. The internet has also enabled the rise of **echo chambers**, where people are exposed primarily to information that reinforces their existing beliefs, and **filter bubbles**, which limit exposure to diverse perspectives. These developments make it all the more important to cultivate strong media literacy skills in the Information Age.

The Importance of Media Literacy in an Age of Misinformation

The Information Age, for all its advantages, has also ushered in an era of **misinformation** and **disinformation**. As the barriers to publishing information have been lowered, the lines between credible journalism, opinion, propaganda, and outright falsehoods have become increasingly blurred. In this environment, the ability to critically evaluate the information we encounter is more important than ever.

Misinformation vs. Disinformation

Before exploring the importance of media literacy, it is essential to understand the difference between **misinformation** and **disinformation**. While both involve the spread of false or misleading information, their intentions differ:

- **Misinformation** refers to incorrect or misleading information that is spread without malicious intent. For example, someone might share an outdated news story or a misunderstanding of a scientific fact without realizing that the information is incorrect.

- **Disinformation**, on the other hand, is deliberately false information spread with the intent to deceive or manipulate. This could include false news stories, conspiracy theories, or propaganda designed to influence public opinion or sow discord.

Both misinformation and disinformation can have serious consequences, especially in the age of social media, where false information can spread rapidly and reach millions of people within minutes. This was evident during major events like the COVID-19 pandemic, where conspiracy theories and misleading medical advice proliferated online, contributing to public confusion and distrust.

The Role of Media Literacy

Media literacy is the ability to access, analyze, evaluate, and create media in a variety of forms. In the digital age, media literacy is an essential skill, as it equips individuals with the tools to navigate the complex information landscape, identify credible sources, and recognize bias, propaganda, and misinformation.

Media literacy involves more than just fact-checking—it encourages a deeper engagement with the content we consume. It teaches us to ask critical questions: Who is the author of this information? What are their credentials? What is the purpose of the message? Is the content based on evidence or opinion? By cultivating these skills, we can become more discerning consumers of information and better equipped to participate in public discourse.

The Dangers of Misinformation

The dangers of misinformation are evident in several areas of modern life, from politics to public health. False information can erode trust in institutions, undermine democratic processes, and even endanger lives.

For example, during the 2016 U.S. presidential election, foreign actors used disinformation campaigns on social media to sow division and influence voters. Fake news stories, conspiracy theories, and misleading political ads were widely shared, contributing to a polarized political environment. Similar tactics have been used in other elections and referendums around the world, raising concerns about the vulnerability of democratic systems in the age of digital media.

Misinformation in public health is particularly dangerous. During the COVID-19 pandemic, false information about the virus, vaccines, and treatments spread rapidly online. Some individuals, influenced by misinformation, refused to follow public health guidelines or declined vaccinations, contributing to higher rates of infection and death. In this context, the ability to identify reliable sources of information and understand scientific evidence became a matter of life and death.

The spread of misinformation is also exacerbated by **social media algorithms**. Platforms like Facebook, Twitter, and YouTube use algorithms that prioritize content based on user engagement, meaning that sensational or emotionally charged content is more likely to be promoted and shared. Unfortunately, false or misleading information often generates more engagement than factual content, leading to the amplification of misinformation.

The Role of Fact-Checking and Critical Thinking

One of the most effective tools for combating misinformation is **fact-checking**. Fact-checking organizations, such as PolitiFact, AFP Fact Check, and FactCheck.org, play a crucial role in verifying the accuracy of information in the media. These organizations assess the veracity of claims made by public figures, news outlets, and social media users, providing a valuable service in an age of widespread misinformation.

However, while fact-checking is important, it is not enough on its own. To navigate the vast sea of information we encounter daily, individuals must also develop strong **critical thinking** skills. Critical thinking involves the ability to analyze information objectively, question assumptions, and draw conclusions based on evidence.

When faced with a piece of information, a critical thinker asks questions like:

- Is this information supported by credible evidence?

- Does the source have a particular bias or agenda?

- Are there alternative perspectives or interpretations of this issue?

- What are the potential consequences of accepting this information as true?

Critical thinking helps us avoid the pitfalls of confirmation bias—the tendency to seek out information that confirms our preexisting beliefs—and encourages us to remain open to new evidence and perspectives. It also helps us recognize the tactics used by purveyors of disinformation, such as fear-mongering, emotional appeals, and cherry-picking data.

How to Critically Assess Sources and Information

In an era where misinformation is widespread, learning how to critically assess sources and information is essential for becoming an informed and responsible global citizen. The following sections offer practical tips for evaluating the credibility of sources and distinguishing between reliable information and misleading or false claims.

1. Evaluate the Source

One of the first steps in assessing information is to evaluate the source. Not all sources are created equal, and some are more reliable than others. When evaluating a source, consider the following questions:

- **Who is the author or publisher?** Check the credentials of the author or organization responsible for the information. Are they an expert in the field? Do they have a history of providing accurate information?

- **What is the reputation of the source?** Established news organizations, academic institutions, and government agencies are generally more reliable than unknown or dubious websites. However, even reputable sources can make mistakes, so it is important to verify information from multiple sources.

- **Is the source biased?** All sources have some degree of bias, but it is important to identify whether the source has a particular agenda or ideological slant. Be cautious of sources that present information in a way that seems intended to provoke an emotional response or confirm your preexisting beliefs.

2. Check for Corroboration

Reliable information is typically corroborated by multiple sources. When you encounter a claim, look for other reputable sources that report the same information. If a piece of information is only reported by one source, especially if that source lacks credibility, it may be false or misleading.

For example, if you read a news story about a major event, such as a natural disaster or political development, check whether other major news outlets are reporting the same story. If reputable sources are not covering the story, it could be a sign that the information is inaccurate or incomplete.

3. Analyze the Evidence

When evaluating information, it is important to distinguish between opinion and evidence. Credible sources back up their claims with facts, data, and research. Be skeptical of sources that make bold claims without providing supporting evidence.

In addition to checking for evidence, consider the quality of the evidence. Is the information based on scientific research, expert testimony, or official data? Or is it based on anecdotal evidence, speculation, or hearsay? High-quality evidence is usually derived from rigorous research methods and peer-reviewed studies, while low-quality evidence is often based on personal opinions or unverified sources.

4. Look for Red Flags

There are certain red flags that can help you identify misinformation or unreliable sources. Be cautious of information that:

- **Relies on sensationalism or fear-mongering.** Misinformation often plays on people's emotions, particularly fear, anger, or outrage. If the information seems designed to provoke an emotional reaction rather than inform, it may be misleading.

- **Lacks transparency.** Credible sources are transparent about where their information comes from. Be wary of sources that do not cite their evidence or provide vague or anonymous sources.

- **Contains logical fallacies.** Logical fallacies are errors in reasoning that undermine the validity of an argument. Common fallacies include ad hominem attacks (attacking the person rather than the argument), false equivalence (comparing two things that are not truly comparable), and straw man arguments (misrepresenting an opponent's argument to make it easier to attack).

5. Stay Informed and Adaptable

Finally, one of the most important aspects of critically assessing information is to stay informed and adaptable. The information landscape is constantly evolving, and new developments in science, politics, and technology can change our understanding of the world. As a result, it is important to remain open to new evidence and willing to adjust your beliefs in light of new information.

Staying informed also means diversifying your sources of information. By exposing yourself to a range of perspectives and viewpoints, you can develop a more nuanced understanding of complex issues and avoid falling into the trap of confirmation bias.

Conclusion

The **Information Age** has transformed the way we access, consume, and share information. While the internet and digital technologies have democratized knowledge and empowered individuals to participate in global conversations, they have also introduced new challenges, particularly in the form of misinformation and disinformation.

In this environment, media literacy is more important than ever. By developing the skills to critically evaluate sources, analyze evidence, and recognize bias, we can navigate the vast and complex information landscape with confidence. History has shown that access to accurate information is essential for the functioning of democratic societies, the advancement of science, and the promotion of human rights.

As we continue to adapt to the realities of the Information Age, let us remember that with the power to access information comes the responsibility to assess it critically. By doing so, we can contribute to a more informed, thoughtful, and connected world.

Chapter 4: The Science of Reality

Science is the pursuit of knowledge and understanding about the natural world. It is a powerful tool for exploring reality, revealing the mechanisms behind the universe, life, and the complexities of human existence. Through the application of the **scientific method**, we can uncover truths about the physical world, test ideas, correct errors, and improve our collective understanding over time.

The impact of science on human life is profound. From the discovery of electricity to the sequencing of the human genome, scientific advancements have continually reshaped our reality. But science is more than a collection of facts and inventions; it's a systematic way of thinking and questioning the world around us.

In this chapter, we will explore the basic principles of the scientific method, how scientific advancements shape our understanding of the universe, and the critical role science plays in addressing global challenges like climate change and disease. Through this exploration, we aim to understand why the science of reality is not only crucial for knowledge but also for the survival and progress of humanity.

Basic Principles of the Scientific Method and Why It Matters

The **scientific method** is a systematic approach to investigating questions about the natural world. At its core, the scientific method is a process of asking questions, forming hypotheses, conducting experiments, and analyzing results to arrive at conclusions. This approach allows scientists to develop an increasingly accurate and comprehensive understanding of the physical and biological systems that govern our world.

The Structure of the Scientific Method

The scientific method is not a rigid set of rules but a flexible, iterative process that involves several key steps:

1. **Observation**: Every scientific inquiry begins with observation. Scientists notice something in the natural world that sparks curiosity—whether it's the way apples fall from trees or the pattern of stars in the night sky.

2. **Question**: Based on their observations, scientists ask questions. For example, Isaac Newton asked why objects fall to the ground, leading him to explore the concept of gravity. Asking questions is a critical part of the scientific process because it defines the direction of inquiry.

3. **Hypothesis**: A hypothesis is a tentative explanation for an observation or phenomenon. It is a prediction that can be tested. A hypothesis must be specific and falsifiable, meaning it can be proven false through experimentation or observation. For instance, Newton's hypothesis might have been that a force (gravity) pulls objects toward the Earth.

4. **Experimentation**: Once a hypothesis is formed, scientists design experiments to test it. Experiments are carefully controlled procedures that allow scientists to isolate variables and measure the outcomes of their tests. For example, Galileo famously dropped spheres of different masses from

the Leaning Tower of Pisa to test his hypothesis about gravity and acceleration.

5. **Data Collection and Analysis**: During an experiment, scientists gather data, which can be qualitative (descriptive) or quantitative (numerical). Analyzing this data allows scientists to determine whether the hypothesis is supported or contradicted by the evidence.

6. **Conclusion**: After analyzing the data, scientists draw conclusions. If the data supports the hypothesis, it is considered valid—though it may still require further testing. If the data contradicts the hypothesis, scientists revise their hypothesis or develop a new one and repeat the process.

7. **Peer Review and Replication**: The scientific method does not end with a single experiment. Scientific findings must be shared with the broader scientific community through peer-reviewed publications. Other scientists then attempt to replicate the results. Replication is essential because it confirms the reliability of the findings.

The strength of the scientific method lies in its iterative nature. Scientific knowledge is not static; it evolves as new evidence emerges, and old ideas are refined or replaced. The process of testing, refining, and retesting hypotheses ensures that science remains dynamic and self-correcting.

Why the Scientific Method Matters

The scientific method is vital for several reasons. First, it provides a systematic way to investigate complex questions about the world. By relying on observation, evidence, and logic, science minimizes the influence of personal biases, emotions, or superstitions. This objectivity is crucial for developing reliable knowledge that can be applied across different contexts.

Second, the scientific method promotes critical thinking. It encourages questioning, skepticism, and curiosity. Rather than accepting ideas at face value, the scientific method challenges us to seek evidence, examine alternatives, and think critically about the information we receive. This approach is not only useful in scientific inquiry but also in everyday decision-making.

Finally, the scientific method has practical applications. From medicine to engineering, scientific discoveries driven by the scientific method have transformed human life. Vaccines, computers, airplanes, and renewable energy technologies all exist because of rigorous scientific investigation. In a world where misinformation and unproven claims are abundant, the scientific method remains one of our best tools for separating fact from fiction.

How Scientific Advancements Shape Our Understanding of the Universe

Science has not only provided us with practical inventions— it has also fundamentally changed how we understand the universe and our place in it. Through centuries of scientific inquiry, we have discovered the laws that govern the cosmos, unraveled the mysteries of life on Earth, and developed the technologies that allow us to explore both the vastness of space and the intricacies of the human genome.

The Structure of the Universe

One of the most profound shifts in human understanding came with the realization that the Earth is not the center of the universe. In ancient times, most people believed in a **geocentric** model, where the Earth was at the center of the cosmos and everything else—planets, stars, and the Sun—revolved around it. This view was upheld for centuries, largely due to the influence of philosophers like Aristotle and the teachings of the Catholic Church.

However, in the 16th century, **Nicolaus Copernicus** proposed a revolutionary idea: the **heliocentric** model. He argued that the Earth and other planets revolved around the Sun. This was a radical departure from the accepted worldview and challenged the prevailing understanding of the universe. Copernicus' model was later supported by the work of **Galileo Galilei** and **Johannes Kepler**, who provided mathematical and observational evidence for a sun-centered solar system. This shift marked the beginning of the **Scientific Revolution**, fundamentally altering our understanding of the universe.

As telescopic technology advanced, scientists discovered more about the nature of the cosmos. **Isaac Newton** developed the theory of gravity, explaining how celestial bodies interact and move in space. Later, in the 20th century, **Albert Einstein**'s theory of **general relativity** further revolutionized our understanding of gravity, time, and space. Relativity revealed that space and time are interconnected and that gravity is the result of the curvature of spacetime caused by mass.

Einstein's work also set the stage for the development of **quantum mechanics**, which explores the behavior of particles at the smallest scales. Quantum mechanics introduced concepts like wave-particle duality and uncertainty, revealing that the universe at the subatomic level is far stranger and less deterministic than classical physics had imagined. These discoveries reshaped not only physics but also philosophy, as they challenged long-held assumptions about the nature of reality.

Today, scientific advancements continue to expand our understanding of the universe. The discovery of **exoplanets** (planets outside our solar system), the mapping of **cosmic microwave background radiation** (the afterglow of the Big Bang), and the study of **dark matter** and **dark energy** are pushing the boundaries of human knowledge. The search for **life on other planets** and the exploration of black holes and neutron stars are among the many frontiers that modern science is investigating. As our understanding of the universe grows, so too does our appreciation for the vastness and complexity of the cosmos.

The Science of Life

In addition to expanding our understanding of the universe, science has transformed our knowledge of life on Earth. One of the most significant scientific advancements in this regard is **Charles Darwin**'s theory of **evolution by natural selection**, published in his 1859 work *On the Origin of Species*. Darwin's theory revolutionized biology by explaining how species change over time in response to environmental pressures. Evolutionary theory provided a unifying framework for understanding the diversity of life on Earth, from the smallest microbes to the largest mammals.

The discovery of **DNA** in the 20th century added a new dimension to our understanding of life. DNA, or deoxyribonucleic acid, is the molecule that carries genetic information in all living organisms. **James Watson** and **Francis Crick**, building on the work of other scientists like **Rosalind Franklin**, determined the double-helix structure of DNA in 1953. This discovery laid the foundation for modern genetics, allowing scientists to study how traits are inherited and how mutations can lead to evolutionary changes.

The sequencing of the **human genome** at the turn of the 21st century was a monumental achievement in biology. It provided a complete map of the genetic instructions that make up a human being, opening the door to advances in medicine, personalized healthcare, and the study of genetic disorders. The field of **genomics** continues to grow, with researchers using genetic information to better understand diseases like cancer and Alzheimer's, as well as exploring the genetic diversity of plants, animals, and microorganisms.

Advances in **biotechnology** and **synthetic biology** are also transforming our understanding of life. Scientists are now able to edit genes using technologies like **CRISPR**, potentially allowing us to cure genetic diseases, modify crops for better resilience, and even create entirely new forms of life in the lab. These developments raise important ethical questions about the limits of human intervention in nature, but they also hold the potential to improve health, food security, and environmental sustainability.

The Cosmos and Our Place in It

The progress of science has not only expanded our knowledge of the physical and biological aspects of reality but has also changed the way we view our place in the universe. As **Carl Sagan** famously said, "We are made of star stuff." This poetic statement captures a profound scientific truth: the elements that make up our bodies—carbon, oxygen, nitrogen—were forged in the hearts of stars billions of years ago. The birth and death of stars, the formation of galaxies, and the vast forces of the cosmos have directly shaped the conditions that allow life to exist on Earth.

In the past, humans often saw themselves as the center of creation, uniquely placed in a universe designed specifically for us. However, modern science has shown that we are one small part of a much larger, more complex, and interconnected universe. The **Big Bang theory**, which explains the origin of the universe, reveals that all matter and energy were once concentrated in a single point before expanding into the cosmos we see today. The universe is still expanding, and galaxies are moving farther apart, driven by the mysterious force of **dark energy**.

As we explore our solar system and beyond, we are constantly reminded of how tiny and fragile our planet is. The images of Earth from space—such as the iconic "**Blue Marble**" photograph taken during the Apollo 17 mission—underscore the unity of life on our planet and the importance of taking care of our home. Science has given us the tools to explore the vastness of space, but it has also deepened our understanding of the need to protect the delicate ecosystems that sustain life on Earth.

The Role of Science in Solving Global Challenges

As humanity faces increasingly complex and interconnected challenges, science plays a critical role in providing solutions. From addressing **climate change** to combating

global diseases, scientific research and technological innovation are essential for navigating the crises that affect our planet and its inhabitants.

Climate Change: Understanding and Mitigating a Global Threat

One of the most pressing challenges of our time is **climate change**. The overwhelming scientific consensus is that human activities, particularly the burning of fossil fuels, are causing global temperatures to rise. This warming is leading to more frequent and severe weather events, rising sea levels, and disruptions to ecosystems. Climate change poses a threat not only to the environment but also to global health, food security, and economic stability.

Science has been at the forefront of understanding the causes and consequences of climate change. Climate scientists use **computer models** and **satellite data** to track changes in the Earth's atmosphere, oceans, and ice caps. These models help predict future climate scenarios based on different levels of greenhouse gas emissions, allowing policymakers to make informed decisions about mitigation strategies.

One of the key scientific tools for addressing climate change is **renewable energy**. Solar, wind, and hydroelectric power offer sustainable alternatives to fossil fuels, reducing carbon emissions and helping transition the world to a low-carbon economy. Advances in **energy storage** and **electric vehicles** are also playing a crucial role in reducing reliance on oil and coal. Meanwhile, research into **carbon capture** and **geoengineering** offers potential solutions for removing carbon dioxide from the atmosphere and mitigating the worst effects of climate change.

However, addressing climate change is not just a scientific challenge—it is also a political and social one. Scientists have provided the evidence, but it is up to governments, businesses, and individuals to take action. International agreements like the **Paris Agreement** aim to limit global warming by reducing emissions, but achieving these goals will require sustained global cooperation and a commitment to science-based policies.

Combating Global Diseases: The Role of Medical Science

Another critical area where science plays a vital role is in **public health**. The COVID-19 pandemic has underscored the importance of scientific research in combating infectious diseases. In a matter of months, scientists were able to identify the virus, sequence its genome, and develop effective vaccines using advanced technologies like **mRNA**. The rapid development and deployment of vaccines were a testament to the power of scientific collaboration and innovation.

Beyond COVID-19, medical science continues to tackle a range of global health challenges, including **HIV/AIDS**, **malaria**, and **tuberculosis**. Advances in **vaccination**, **antibiotics**, and **antiviral therapies** have saved millions of lives, and ongoing research in areas like **immunotherapy** and **genetic medicine** promises to revolutionize healthcare in the coming decades.

One of the most promising areas of medical science is the development of **personalized medicine**. By studying an individual's genetic makeup, doctors can tailor treatments to the specific needs of each patient, improving outcomes and reducing side effects. Advances in **artificial intelligence** (AI) and **machine learning** are also helping doctors diagnose diseases more accurately and develop new treatment protocols based on vast amounts of patient data.

However, science alone cannot solve global health challenges. Public health initiatives, education, and access to healthcare are equally important. The fight against diseases requires a coordinated effort between scientists, healthcare providers, governments, and communities.

Scientific Solutions for Sustainable Development

In addition to climate change and public health, science plays a critical role in addressing other global challenges related to **sustainable development**. The United Nations' **Sustainable Development Goals (SDGs)** highlight the importance of scientific research and innovation in areas such as clean water, food security, and energy access.

For example, advances in **agriculture** are helping farmers grow more food with fewer resources. **Genetically modified crops** (GMOs), improved irrigation techniques, and **precision farming** technologies are increasing yields and reducing the environmental impact of agriculture. Meanwhile, research into **alternative proteins** and **lab-grown meat** could help address the environmental and ethical concerns associated with traditional livestock farming.

In the area of **water management**, science is developing technologies to desalinate seawater, purify wastewater, and improve irrigation systems to conserve water in drought-prone regions. These innovations are essential for ensuring that the world's growing population has access to clean and reliable sources of water.

Science also plays a key role in **conservation efforts,** helping protect biodiversity and ecosystems from human activities. Ecologists use data from field studies, satellite imagery, and genetic research to understand how species interact with their environments and how ecosystems can be preserved. Conservation science informs policies on endangered species, deforestation, and habitat restoration, helping mitigate the impact of human activities on the natural world.

Conclusion

Science is not only a tool for understanding reality—it is a method of shaping the future. From uncovering the mysteries of the cosmos to solving pressing global challenges, the scientific method provides humanity with a reliable, evidence-based framework for making informed decisions.

In this chapter, we have explored the basic principles of the scientific method and its importance in shaping our understanding of the universe. We have seen how scientific advancements have changed the way we view reality, from the structure of the cosmos to the intricacies of life on Earth. Finally, we have examined the critical role science plays in addressing global challenges such as climate change, disease, and sustainable development.

The science of reality is not a static body of knowledge but a dynamic process that continues to evolve. As new discoveries are made and new technologies are developed, our understanding of the world deepens. In the Information Age, where misinformation and disinformation can easily spread, science provides a beacon of truth and a method for separating fact from fiction.

As we move forward, it is crucial that we embrace science not only as a tool for solving problems but as a way of thinking critically, questioning assumptions, and seeking out the evidence needed to navigate an increasingly complex world. Through science, we can continue to expand our understanding of reality, address the challenges facing our planet, and ensure a better future for generations to come.

Chapter 5: The Economic Forces Shaping the World

Economics plays a critical role in shaping the world we live in, influencing everything from the wealth of nations to the day-to-day lives of individuals. It touches on the distribution of resources, the production of goods, the flow of capital, and the policies that govern these processes. Understanding economics is essential to making sense of the forces that drive human behavior, the structure of societies, and the relationships between nations.

This chapter provides an introduction to global economics, explaining how economic forces influence societies and the lives of people around the world. We will explore core economic concepts like **supply and demand**, **globalization**, and **capitalism**, as well as discuss the profound impact of **wealth inequality** and **economic policies** on different societies. By understanding these economic forces, we can gain insights into why some societies prosper while others struggle, how decisions made by governments and corporations affect everyday life, and how global economic trends influence local realities.

An Introduction to Global Economics and How They Influence Society

At its core, economics is about how societies allocate scarce resources to meet the needs and desires of people. These resources include natural resources like land and water, human resources like labor and knowledge, and capital resources like machinery and money. The study of economics seeks to understand how these resources are used, how wealth is created and distributed, and how individuals and governments make choices in the face of scarcity.

The Importance of Economics in Society

Economics is often described as the "science of decision-making," and its principles are applied not only in markets but also in government policies, international relations, and personal choices. The decisions made by policymakers, businesses, and consumers affect not just individuals but also the broader society. For example, a government's decision to lower interest rates can encourage borrowing and investment, stimulating economic growth. Similarly, a company's decision to outsource manufacturing to another country can create jobs abroad while causing job losses at home.

Economic forces are present in every aspect of life. From the price of food at the grocery store to the availability of healthcare, education, and housing, economics determines the accessibility and affordability of goods and services. The wealth of a nation, the unemployment rate, inflation, and international trade relations are all governed by economic principles.

Because of its pervasive influence, economics is often described as the backbone of society. A healthy, well-managed economy can lead to widespread prosperity, higher living standards, and social stability. Conversely, a poorly managed economy can lead to poverty, unemployment, and social unrest.

Microeconomics vs. Macroeconomics

Economics can be broadly divided into two fields: **microeconomics** and **macroeconomics**. Each field focuses on different levels of economic activity, though they are deeply interconnected.

- **Microeconomics** deals with individual decision-making units, such as consumers, workers, and businesses. It examines how these units interact in markets to determine the price of goods and services, how resources are allocated, and how supply and demand affect market outcomes. For example, microeconomics might explore how a company decides the price of its product based on consumer demand or how a worker chooses between different job offers based on wages and working conditions.

- **Macroeconomics**, on the other hand, looks at the economy as a whole. It focuses on aggregate economic phenomena, such as national income, unemployment, inflation, and economic growth. Macroeconomists study how policies, such as government spending and taxation, impact the overall economy. For instance, macroeconomics would analyze how a country's decision to invest in infrastructure could stimulate job creation and economic growth or how an economic recession could lead to higher unemployment rates.

Both microeconomics and macroeconomics are essential for understanding how economies function. While microeconomics provides insights into how individuals and businesses make choices, macroeconomics allows us to understand large-scale economic trends and the role of government in managing the economy.

Understanding Concepts Like Supply and Demand, Globalization, and Capitalism

To understand how economic forces shape the world, it is essential to grasp a few fundamental concepts that underpin modern economies. **Supply and demand**, **globalization**, and **capitalism** are key ideas that help explain how goods and services are produced, distributed, and consumed.

Supply and Demand: The Forces that Drive Markets

One of the most basic and powerful concepts in economics is **supply and demand**. These two forces determine the price of goods and services in a market economy, guiding the allocation of resources.

- **Supply** refers to the quantity of a good or service that producers are willing to offer at various price levels. Typically, as the price of a product rises, producers are willing to supply more of it because higher prices lead to higher profits.

- **Demand**, on the other hand, refers to the quantity of a good or service that consumers are willing to purchase at different prices. In general, as the price of a product decreases, demand increases because more people are able to afford the product.

The relationship between supply and demand creates what is known as **market equilibrium**, the point where the quantity supplied matches the quantity demanded. At this point, the market clears, meaning there is no surplus or shortage of goods. Prices naturally adjust to bring supply and demand into balance. For example, if there is a sudden shortage of oil, the price of oil will rise, encouraging producers to supply more oil and consumers to use less, eventually restoring equilibrium.

Supply and demand are dynamic forces, constantly shifting in response to changes in technology, consumer preferences, and external factors like natural disasters or geopolitical events. For example, the COVID-19 pandemic disrupted global supply chains, leading to shortages of various products and pushing prices higher in many sectors.

Globalization: Connecting Economies and Societies

Globalization refers to the increasing interconnectedness of economies, cultures, and societies around the world. It is driven by advances in technology, transportation, and communication, which have made it easier for goods, services, and ideas to flow across borders. As a result, the world economy has become more integrated, with countries relying on one another for trade, investment, and labor.

Globalization has had profound effects on economies and societies. On the one hand, it has enabled countries to specialize in producing goods and services where they have a comparative advantage, leading to more efficient resource use and lower prices for consumers. For example, countries like China have become manufacturing powerhouses, producing goods that are sold all over the world at competitive prices. In return, countries like the United States and Germany export high-tech products and services to global markets.

On the other hand, globalization has also led to the outsourcing of jobs, particularly in manufacturing, from developed countries to developing ones where labor is cheaper. This has created economic opportunities in some countries but has also led to job losses and economic dislocation in others. The global financial crisis of 2008, which was triggered by the collapse of the U.S. housing market, demonstrated how interconnected the world's economies have become. The crisis quickly spread to other parts of the world, leading to a global recession.

Globalization has also facilitated the spread of ideas, cultures, and technologies. The internet, for example, has created a global platform for the exchange of information and innovation. However, globalization is not without its challenges. It has contributed to the rise of **income inequality**, as some countries and individuals have benefited more than others. Additionally, globalization has raised concerns about the environment, as increased production and transportation have led to higher carbon emissions and the depletion of natural resources.

Capitalism: The Dominant Economic System

Capitalism is the dominant economic system in most parts of the world today. It is characterized by private ownership of the means of production, market-based resource allocation, and the pursuit of profit. In a capitalist economy, businesses and individuals are free to compete with one another to produce goods and services, and prices are determined by supply and demand.

One of the strengths of capitalism is its ability to drive innovation and economic growth. Competition among businesses encourages efficiency, productivity, and the development of new technologies. Entrepreneurs, motivated by the potential for profit, take risks to create new products and services that improve people's lives. For example, the development of the smartphone, which has transformed communication and commerce around the world, was driven by competition among technology companies in a capitalist system.

However, capitalism also has its drawbacks. One of the most significant criticisms of capitalism is that it can lead to **wealth inequality**, with a small number of individuals and corporations accumulating a disproportionate share of wealth and power. This concentration of wealth can lead to social and political instability, as those who are left behind may feel marginalized and disenfranchised.

Another criticism of capitalism is that it tends to prioritize short-term profits over long-term social and environmental sustainability. In the pursuit of profit, businesses may exploit workers, degrade the environment, or engage in practices that harm communities. This has led to calls for greater government regulation and oversight of markets, as well as the development of alternative economic models, such as **socialism** and **cooperative economics**, which emphasize collective ownership and resource-sharing.

Despite these criticisms, capitalism remains the dominant economic system worldwide, shaping the way resources are allocated and wealth is distributed. Understanding how capitalism works, and its impact on society, is essential for making sense of the economic forces that shape our world.

The Impact of Wealth Inequality and Economic Policies on Different Societies

One of the most pressing issues in global economics today is **wealth inequality**. The gap between the richest and the poorest individuals and countries has widened significantly in recent decades, leading to a range of social, political, and economic challenges. In this section, we will explore the causes and consequences of wealth inequality, as well as the role of **economic policies** in addressing or exacerbating these disparities.

Wealth Inequality: Causes and Consequences

Wealth inequality refers to the unequal distribution of assets, income, and opportunities among individuals and groups within a society or between nations. While some degree of inequality is inevitable in any economy, extreme inequality can have negative consequences for both individuals and societies.

One of the primary drivers of wealth inequality is the **unequal distribution of capital**. In capitalist economies, those who own capital—such as land, businesses, stocks, and real estate—have the ability to generate wealth through investment and the accumulation of profits. Those who do not own capital, particularly workers, are limited to earning wages, which may not increase as rapidly as the returns on capital. This creates a feedback loop, where the rich become richer through investment, while the poor and middle class struggle to accumulate wealth.

Another driver of inequality is **technological change**. Advances in technology, particularly automation and artificial intelligence, have transformed industries and labor markets. While these technologies have increased productivity and economic growth, they have also displaced many low-skilled workers, leading to higher unemployment and wage stagnation in certain sectors. At the same time, high-skilled workers, particularly those in technology and finance, have seen their incomes rise, exacerbating income inequality.

Globalization has also contributed to wealth inequality. While it has lifted millions of people out of poverty in developing countries by providing access to new markets and jobs, it has also widened the gap between the rich and poor in developed countries. In many cases, the benefits of globalization have accrued disproportionately to the wealthy, particularly multinational corporations and investors, while workers in industries like manufacturing have faced job losses and wage stagnation.

The consequences of wealth inequality are far-reaching. Economically, inequality can lead to slower growth, as the middle and working classes, who tend to spend a larger portion of their income, have less purchasing power. Socially, inequality can lead to political instability, as those who feel left behind may turn to populist or extremist movements. Additionally, inequality can undermine social cohesion and trust, as individuals in unequal societies may feel less connected to their communities and more isolated from one another.

Economic Policies: Shaping Wealth and Opportunity

Governments play a crucial role in shaping the distribution of wealth and opportunities within a society through **economic policies**. These policies, which include taxation, social welfare programs, education, healthcare, and labor regulations, can either mitigate or exacerbate wealth inequality.

- **Taxation**: Tax policies are one of the most direct ways that governments can influence wealth distribution. **Progressive tax systems**, where higher-income individuals pay a larger percentage of their income in taxes, can help reduce inequality by redistributing wealth from the rich to the poor. In contrast, **regressive tax systems**, where lower-income individuals pay a larger share of their income, can worsen inequality. Tax policies that offer generous deductions or loopholes for corporations and the wealthy can further entrench wealth disparities.

- **Social Welfare Programs**: Social safety nets, such as unemployment benefits, healthcare subsidies, and food assistance, are designed to provide support for individuals and families in need. These programs can help reduce poverty and inequality by ensuring that all citizens have access to basic services and opportunities. Countries with strong social welfare systems, such as those in Scandinavia, tend to have lower levels of inequality and higher levels of social mobility.

- **Education and Healthcare**: Access to quality education and healthcare is essential for creating equal opportunities. Governments that invest in public education and healthcare systems can help ensure that all citizens, regardless of their socioeconomic background, have the chance to succeed. In contrast, societies where education and healthcare are largely privatized and expensive may see greater inequality, as the wealthy can afford better services, while the poor are left behind.

- **Labor Regulations**: Labor laws, such as minimum wage legislation, workers' rights protections, and collective bargaining rights, play a critical role in determining the distribution of income between workers and employers. Countries with stronger labor protections tend to have lower levels of income inequality, as workers are able to negotiate for fair wages and working conditions. In contrast, countries with weak labor laws may see rising inequality as wages stagnate and worker protections erode.

In recent years, there has been growing debate about the role of **universal basic income** (UBI) as a potential solution to wealth inequality. UBI is a policy in which the government provides all citizens with a regular, unconditional cash payment. Proponents argue that UBI could provide a financial safety net in an era of automation and job displacement, while critics argue that it could be too costly or reduce incentives to work. The concept has gained traction in countries like Finland, where pilot programs have been implemented to test its effectiveness.

Global Inequality: The North-South Divide

Wealth inequality is not only an issue within countries but also between countries. The **Global North**, which includes wealthy, industrialized countries in North America, Europe, and parts of Asia, is significantly richer than the **Global South**, which includes developing countries in Africa, Latin America, and parts of Asia. This disparity is often referred to as the **North-South divide**.

The roots of global inequality can be traced to historical factors, such as **colonialism** and **imperialism**, which allowed European powers to extract resources and wealth from their colonies. Even after the end of colonialism, many countries in the Global South have struggled to overcome the legacies of exploitation, underdevelopment, and economic dependence on the Global North.

Today, global inequality is perpetuated by a range of factors, including unequal access to education, healthcare, and infrastructure, as well as unfair trade practices and debt burdens. While globalization has provided some countries in the Global South with economic opportunities, many others have been left behind. The COVID-19 pandemic further highlighted global inequalities, as wealthy countries were able to secure vaccines and economic relief more quickly than poorer nations.

International organizations, such as the **World Bank**, the **International Monetary Fund (IMF)**, and the **United Nations**, play a role in addressing global inequality by providing financial assistance, promoting economic development, and advocating for fairer trade practices. However, critics argue that these institutions often promote policies that benefit wealthy countries and multinational corporations at the expense of poorer nations.

Efforts to reduce global inequality include initiatives like **fair trade**, which aims to ensure that producers in developing countries receive fair prices for their goods, and **debt relief**, which seeks to alleviate the burden of debt on impoverished nations. However, achieving true global equity will require a comprehensive approach that addresses both the historical causes and the modern drivers of inequality.

Conclusion

The economic forces shaping the world are vast and complex, influencing every aspect of life, from individual decisions to global politics. By understanding the core concepts of **supply and demand**, **globalization**, and

capitalism, we gain insight into how markets function and how wealth is created and distributed. However, the economic landscape is also shaped by deeper forces, such as **wealth inequality** and **economic policies**, which determine who benefits from economic growth and who is left behind.

As we look to the future, it is clear that addressing the challenges of wealth inequality, both within and between nations, will be essential for creating a more just and sustainable world. Governments, businesses, and individuals must work together to ensure that the benefits of economic growth are shared more equitably and that all people have access to the opportunities and resources they need to thrive.

Economics is not just a theoretical field—it is a practical and essential tool for understanding the world. By studying the economic forces that shape society, we can better understand the challenges and opportunities facing humanity and make informed decisions about the future of our world.

Chapter 6: Politics and Power Dynamics

Politics is the mechanism through which societies make collective decisions, allocate resources, and maintain social order. It is inseparable from power—who holds it, how it is exercised, and for whose benefit. Across the globe, political systems and governance structures vary widely, yet they all influence how societies function and how individuals relate to the state and each other. Whether in democratic societies, authoritarian regimes, or somewhere in between, politics shapes the lives of individuals and communities in profound ways.

This chapter delves into the fundamental elements of politics and power dynamics. We will explore how different political systems and governance structures work, examine the role of power and influence in shaping societies and international relations, and discuss the importance of civic engagement and understanding political structures. By understanding these dimensions, we can better navigate the political forces that shape our world and become more informed, engaged citizens.

How Political Systems and Governance Structures Work Globally

Political systems are the frameworks that define how governments are organized and how power is distributed within a society. These systems differ in terms of who holds power, how leaders are chosen, and the relationship between the state and the people. While no political system is perfect, each one reflects the unique history, culture, and values of the society it governs.

Democracy: Rule by the People

Democracy is one of the most widely recognized forms of government, characterized by the participation of citizens in the decision-making process. In a democratic system, power is vested in the people, who exercise that power either directly or through elected representatives. The defining features of democracy include free and fair elections, the protection of individual rights and liberties, and the rule of law.

Democracies can take many forms, but they generally fall into two categories:

- **Direct Democracy**: In a direct democracy, citizens participate in the decision-making process directly, without intermediaries. This form of government is rare in modern times, but it existed in ancient Athens, where citizens gathered to vote on laws and policies. In contemporary societies, direct democracy is sometimes used at the local level or through mechanisms like referendums, where citizens vote directly on specific issues.

- **Representative Democracy**: In most modern democracies, citizens elect representatives to make decisions on their behalf. These representatives are accountable to the people through regular elections. Representative democracies can be further divided into **parliamentary** and **presidential** systems. In parliamentary systems, the executive branch (the prime minister and the cabinet) is drawn from the legislature, while in presidential systems, the executive (the president) is separate from the legislative branch.

In democracies, political parties play a crucial role by organizing candidates for elections, advocating for specific policies, and providing voters with choices. Democratic systems rely on **checks and balances** to prevent the concentration of power in any one branch of government. Independent judiciaries, free press, and civil society organizations are essential components of a healthy democracy, ensuring that the government remains accountable to the people.

Authoritarianism: Centralized Control

Authoritarianism is a form of government in which power is concentrated in the hands of a single leader or a small group of elites. In contrast to democracies, authoritarian regimes often suppress political opposition, limit individual freedoms, and exercise control over many aspects of public and private life. Decisions are typically made by the ruling party or leader without meaningful input from the public.

There are several types of authoritarian systems, including:

- **Dictatorships**: In a dictatorship, one person holds absolute power over the state. This power is often maintained through coercion, propaganda, and the suppression of dissent. Dictatorships can be military-based, where leaders come to power through force, or civilian, where a political leader consolidates control.

- **Monarchies**: Some authoritarian regimes are monarchies, where a king or queen holds significant or absolute power. In **absolute monarchies**, the monarch has unchecked authority, as seen in countries like Saudi Arabia. In contrast, **constitutional monarchies**—such as the United

Kingdom or Japan—limit the monarch's powers, with real political authority vested in elected representatives.

- **One-Party States**: In one-party states, a single political party controls the government, and other parties are either banned or severely restricted. Examples include **China**, where the Communist Party holds power, and **Cuba**, where the Communist Party governs without competition. One-party states often use state-controlled media and censorship to maintain their hold on power.

Authoritarian regimes typically use various tools to maintain control, such as **state surveillance**, **censorship**, and **propaganda**. While some authoritarian leaders justify their rule by claiming they bring stability or economic development, the lack of accountability and restrictions on political participation often lead to abuses of power.

Hybrid Regimes and Illiberal Democracies

Between democratic and authoritarian systems lies a spectrum of **hybrid regimes** and **illiberal democracies**, where elements of both democracy and authoritarianism coexist. These regimes may hold elections, but they often lack key democratic features like free press, independent judiciaries, or civil liberties. Leaders in these systems may be elected, but they often manipulate the electoral process or undermine democratic institutions to maintain power.

Illiberal democracies, for example, may have regular elections, but the rights and freedoms of citizens are curtailed. **Hungary** under Prime Minister Viktor Orbán and **Turkey** under President Recep Tayyip Erdoğan are often cited as examples of illiberal democracies, where leaders have used democratic mechanisms to gain power but then weakened democratic institutions to entrench their rule.

In hybrid regimes, the appearance of democracy masks the reality of centralized power and limited political competition. These regimes pose significant challenges to the global trend toward democratization and raise important questions about the health of democracy in the 21st century.

The Role of Power and Influence in Shaping Societies and International Relations

At the heart of politics is **power**—the ability to influence or control the actions of others. Power dynamics exist at every level of society, from local communities to international relations. Understanding how power is distributed and exercised is essential for comprehending the political forces that shape societies and determine the course of global events.

The Nature of Political Power

Political power can be defined as the capacity to make decisions that affect the lives of individuals and groups. This power can take many forms, from **coercion** (using force or threats to achieve compliance) to **influence** (shaping people's beliefs or actions through persuasion). Power can be exercised through formal institutions, such as governments and legal systems, or informally, through networks of influence, culture, and ideology.

One of the key distinctions in the study of power is between **hard power** and **soft power**:

- **Hard Power**: Hard power refers to the use of force, coercion, or economic pressure to achieve political goals. Military intervention, economic sanctions, and coercive diplomacy are examples of hard power. Historically, empires and nation-states have relied on hard power to expand their influence, conquer territory, or defend their interests. In contemporary international relations, hard power remains important, particularly for superpowers like the United States, China, and Russia.

- **Soft Power**: Soft power, a term coined by political scientist **Joseph Nye**, refers to the ability to shape the preferences and behaviors of others through attraction and persuasion rather than force. Cultural diplomacy, media influence, and the promotion of values such as democracy, human rights, and freedom are examples of soft power. Countries like the United States and the United Kingdom have historically used soft power to project their cultural influence globally, through Hollywood films, universities, and international aid programs. Soft power is often seen as a more sustainable and ethical form of influence than hard power, though it is no less strategic.

In addition to hard and soft power, **economic power** plays a significant role in shaping both domestic and international politics. Wealthier countries and corporations often wield disproportionate influence in global institutions like the **World Trade Organization (WTO)**, the **International Monetary Fund (IMF)**, and the **World Bank**, shaping policies that affect global trade, development, and financial stability.

Power and Social Structure: Class, Race, and Gender

Power is not only a feature of international relations but also shapes the internal dynamics of societies. Power imbalances based on **class**, **race**, **gender**, and **ethnicity** play a central role in determining access to resources, political representation, and opportunities.

Class-based power refers to the ways in which wealth and economic status affect one's access to political influence. In capitalist societies, wealthier individuals and corporations often have more political influence than those with less economic power. For example, wealthy individuals and interest groups may use their resources to fund political campaigns, lobby for favorable policies, or influence public opinion through media ownership.

Racial and ethnic power dynamics are also significant in shaping political systems and societies. Throughout history, systems of racial hierarchy, such as apartheid in South Africa or Jim Crow laws in the United States, have been used to exclude marginalized racial and ethnic groups from political participation and economic opportunities. Even in contemporary societies, racial and ethnic minorities often face systemic barriers to political representation, equal treatment under the law, and access to economic resources.

Gender-based power dynamics affect women's access to political and economic power. While progress has been made toward gender equality in many parts of the world, women remain underrepresented in political leadership and decision-making positions globally. **Patriarchy**—a system in which men hold disproportionate power—continues to shape political institutions, economic systems, and social norms. Feminist movements around the world advocate for gender equality and challenge systems of power that disadvantage women and other gender minorities.

Understanding how power operates within societies is crucial for addressing inequality, promoting social justice, and ensuring that all individuals have access to political representation and opportunities.

International Relations and the Balance of Power

At the global level, **international relations** are shaped by the distribution of power among states. The concept of the **balance of power** refers to the idea that no single state should dominate the international system. Historically, the balance of power has been maintained through alliances, diplomacy, and, at times, war.

In the post-World War II era, the global balance of power was defined by the **Cold War**, a geopolitical struggle between the United States and the Soviet Union. This period was characterized by intense rivalry, military buildup, and the formation of alliances, such as **NATO** (North Atlantic Treaty Organization) and the **Warsaw Pact**. While the Cold War ended with the collapse of the Soviet Union in 1991, the balance of power continues to shape international relations.

In the 21st century, new dynamics are emerging in the global balance of power. The rise of **China** as an economic and military power, along with the resurgence of **Russia** and the influence of regional powers like **India**, **Brazil**, and **Turkey**, is challenging the unipolar dominance of the United States. At the same time, non-state actors, such as multinational corporations, international organizations, and terrorist groups, are playing an increasingly important role in global politics.

International relations are also shaped by **geopolitical competition** over resources, territory, and influence. For example, conflicts over access to oil, natural gas, and other resources have driven international tensions and military interventions. The strategic importance of regions like the Middle East, the South China Sea, and the Arctic has made them focal points for geopolitical rivalry.

The future of international relations will likely be influenced by new challenges, such as **climate change**, **cybersecurity**, and **pandemics**, which require global cooperation and a rethinking of traditional power dynamics. Understanding how power operates at the international level is essential for addressing these global challenges and promoting peace and stability in an increasingly interconnected world.

The Importance of Civic Engagement and Understanding Political Structures

In any society, the participation of citizens in the political process is essential for ensuring accountability, protecting rights, and promoting the common good. **Civic engagement** refers to the ways in which individuals and communities participate in political and social life, whether through voting, activism, volunteering, or advocacy.

The Role of Voting in Democracy

In democratic societies, voting is one of the most fundamental forms of civic engagement. Elections provide citizens with the opportunity to choose their leaders and influence government policies. While voting may seem like a simple act, it is the cornerstone of representative democracy. Through the electoral process, citizens hold their leaders accountable and ensure that their voices are heard.

However, not all citizens have equal access to the voting process. In many parts of the world, **voter suppression**, **disenfranchisement**, and **gerrymandering**—the manipulation of electoral districts for political advantage—undermine the democratic process. In some countries, political elites use legal and extralegal means to prevent marginalized groups, such as racial and ethnic minorities or the poor, from voting. Ensuring fair and free elections is critical to maintaining the integrity of democracy.

Civic Engagement Beyond Voting

While voting is an important form of civic engagement, it is by no means the only way that citizens can participate in politics. **Activism**, **advocacy**, and **community organizing** are powerful tools for shaping political outcomes and holding governments accountable. Throughout history, social movements—from the civil rights movement in the United States to the anti-apartheid movement in South Africa—have played a crucial role in bringing about political change.

In addition to traditional forms of civic engagement, new technologies and social media have created opportunities for digital activism and online advocacy. Platforms like Twitter, Facebook, and Instagram allow individuals to organize protests, raise awareness about social issues, and mobilize supporters. The global reach of social media has given rise to new forms of political participation, enabling people to engage with political movements and causes around the world.

Civic engagement is not limited to politics at the national level. **Local politics**—such as city councils, school boards, and neighborhood associations—offer opportunities for citizens to influence decisions that directly affect their communities. Engaging in local politics can have a significant impact on issues like housing, education, transportation, and public safety.

Understanding Political Structures and Institutions

To engage effectively in politics, it is important to understand how political structures and institutions work. Political structures include the **executive**, **legislative**, and **judicial** branches of government, as well as local and regional authorities. Each branch of government has specific responsibilities, and the relationship between these branches is often governed by a system of **checks and balances**, designed to prevent the concentration of power.

- The **executive branch** is responsible for implementing and enforcing laws. In presidential systems, the president is the head of the executive branch, while in parliamentary systems, the prime minister holds this position. The executive branch also includes government agencies and ministries that oversee areas such as defense, health, education, and foreign affairs.

- The **legislative branch** is responsible for making laws and representing the interests of the people. In democracies, the legislative branch is typically composed of elected representatives, such as members of parliament or congress. The legislative process involves debating, amending, and passing bills, which are then implemented by the executive branch.

- The **judicial branch** interprets and enforces the laws of the country. Courts and judges play a critical role in ensuring that laws are applied fairly and consistently. In some countries, constitutional courts have the power to strike down laws that violate the constitution, serving as a check on the legislative and executive branches.

Understanding how these institutions work is essential for effective civic engagement. Citizens who are informed about political structures can hold their leaders accountable, advocate for policies that benefit their communities, and ensure that their rights are protected.

Conclusion

Politics and power dynamics are fundamental forces shaping the world we live in. From the design of political systems to the exercise of power within societies and on the global stage, politics influences every aspect of human life. Understanding how political systems function, how power is distributed, and how individuals and communities can engage with political structures is essential for making sense of the world.

Whether in democratic societies, authoritarian regimes, or hybrid systems, the distribution of power determines who has access to resources, who makes decisions, and who benefits from policies. By examining the role of power and influence, we can better understand the challenges of governance, social justice, and international relations.

Most importantly, civic engagement is the lifeblood of healthy political systems. When citizens actively participate in the political process, whether through voting, activism, or community involvement, they contribute to the creation of a more just and equitable society. In an increasingly complex and interconnected world, understanding politics and power dynamics is not only a matter of knowledge but also a matter of empowerment. By engaging with political structures, we can shape the future of our communities, nations, and the world.

Chapter 7: Culture and Identity

Culture is one of the most powerful forces shaping human life. It influences how we see the world, how we relate to others, and even how we understand ourselves. From the values we hold to the languages we speak, our sense of personal and collective identity is intricately linked to the cultural environment in which we grow and live. Culture serves as both a lens through which we perceive reality and a set of practices, customs, and traditions that define our place in society.

This chapter explores the role of culture in shaping personal and collective identities, examines the deep relationship between language, religion, and tradition, and discusses the importance of cultural exchange in today's globalized world. By understanding the ways in which culture and identity interact, we can gain a deeper appreciation of the diversity of human experience and develop a more nuanced understanding of the forces that shape our identities.

How Culture Shapes Personal and Collective Identities

Identity refers to the way individuals see themselves and are perceived by others. It encompasses personal characteristics, such as beliefs, values, and personality traits, as well as social affiliations, such as nationality, ethnicity, gender, and religion. **Culture**, in turn, plays a key role in shaping these identities by providing the framework through which individuals understand their place in the world.

Personal Identity: Culture as a Mirror

Personal identity is deeply influenced by the cultural environment in which a person is raised. From an early age, individuals are socialized into the norms, values, and practices of their culture. These cultural elements help to shape one's sense of self, influencing everything from beliefs and behaviors to aspirations and worldviews. The stories we are told, the traditions we observe, and the symbols we encounter all contribute to how we construct our personal identity.

For instance, in individualistic cultures—such as those found in many Western nations—people are often encouraged to prioritize personal autonomy, self-expression, and individual achievement. From an early age, children in these societies may be taught that success and fulfillment come from personal initiative and independence. This emphasis on individuality shapes how people in these cultures understand their sense of self, leading them to define themselves in terms of personal goals, ambitions, and accomplishments.

In contrast, in more **collectivist cultures**—found in many parts of Asia, Africa, and Latin America—individuals may be encouraged to view themselves primarily in relation to their family, community, or social group. In these societies, values like social harmony, loyalty, and interdependence are often emphasized. A person's identity is less about individual achievement and more about fulfilling social roles and contributing to the well-being of the group. As a result, people raised in collectivist cultures may define their identity in terms of their relationships and responsibilities to others.

These cultural distinctions are not absolute, and people's identities are shaped by a wide range of factors beyond culture. However, the cultural context provides the foundation upon which personal identity is built, influencing how individuals understand themselves and their place in the world.

Collective Identity: Culture as a Unifying Force

While personal identity refers to how individuals see themselves, **collective identity** refers to how groups define themselves as distinct from others. Collective identities are often based on shared characteristics, such as ethnicity, nationality, religion, or language, and they provide individuals with a sense of belonging and connection to a larger community.

Culture plays a critical role in shaping collective identities by providing the shared symbols, narratives, and practices that bind people together. **National identity**, for example, is often shaped by a shared history, language, and set of cultural practices that distinguish one nation from another. People in a given country may feel a strong sense of unity based on these shared cultural elements, even if they come from different regions or backgrounds. National holidays, historical commemorations, and national symbols, such as flags and anthems, all serve to reinforce this sense of collective identity.

Similarly, **ethnic identity** is shaped by shared cultural traditions, customs, and experiences that differentiate one ethnic group from others. For example, many Indigenous communities around the world maintain a strong sense of ethnic identity through the preservation of their languages, oral traditions, and rituals. These cultural practices provide a sense of continuity with the past and a collective sense of belonging in the present.

Religious identity is another powerful form of collective identity, often shaped by shared beliefs, rituals, and values.

Religious communities, whether small or global in scope, provide individuals with a sense of connection to something greater than themselves, often transcending national or ethnic boundaries. For many people, their religious identity is a central part of who they are, informing their moral values, social behavior, and worldview.

Collective identities are not static; they evolve over time in response to changing social, political, and economic conditions. Globalization, migration, and technological change, for example, have led to the creation of **hybrid identities**—where individuals draw on multiple cultural influences to define themselves. In an increasingly interconnected world, many people navigate multiple identities, balancing their national, ethnic, religious, or linguistic identities in complex and dynamic ways.

Exploring the Relationship Between Language, Religion, and Tradition

Three core elements of culture—**language**, **religion**, and **tradition**—are intimately connected to the formation of both personal and collective identities. These cultural elements provide individuals with the tools to express their beliefs, values, and sense of belonging. They also serve as carriers of history, memory, and meaning, shaping how communities define themselves across generations.

Language: The Foundation of Identity and Communication

Language is one of the most powerful markers of identity. It is not only a tool for communication but also a key element in the construction of both personal and collective identity.

The language we speak shapes how we see the world, how we relate to others, and how we express our thoughts and emotions.

At the individual level, the language or languages a person speaks are often tied to their sense of self. For bilingual or multilingual individuals, language can be a way of navigating different cultural worlds. People may choose to speak different languages in different contexts, expressing different aspects of their identity depending on the social setting. For example, someone may speak their native language at home to maintain a connection with their cultural heritage, while using another language in public or professional settings.

At the collective level, language is a central component of **cultural identity**. Entire communities are often defined by the language they speak, and the preservation of a language is often seen as vital to the survival of a culture. Many Indigenous communities around the world place a high value on language preservation, recognizing that their languages carry not only linguistic meaning but also cultural knowledge, oral histories, and spiritual traditions. The loss of a language is often seen as a loss of cultural identity, as it represents the erosion of the unique worldview that the language embodies.

Language is also a powerful tool for social and political organization. National languages, for example, are often promoted as symbols of national unity, while minority languages may face suppression or marginalization in favor of the dominant language. In many cases, linguistic identity becomes a point of contention in political struggles for recognition and autonomy.

In addition, language shapes how we perceive the world. The **Sapir-Whorf hypothesis**, or **linguistic relativity**, suggests that the structure of a language influences its speakers' worldview. For example, some languages have multiple words to describe specific colors or concepts, while others may have none, leading to differences in perception and cognition. While this hypothesis remains debated, it highlights the idea that language is not just a neutral medium of communication but a force that actively shapes human thought and culture.

Religion: A Source of Meaning and Morality

Religion is another key cultural force that shapes both personal and collective identities. For many people, religion provides a sense of purpose, community, and moral guidance. It is often closely tied to cultural traditions, shaping everything from social norms to legal systems.

At the personal level, religious beliefs can form the core of an individual's identity. People who adhere to a particular faith may see their religious beliefs as integral to their sense of self, shaping how they make decisions, how they interact with others, and how they find meaning in life. For example, a person's religious beliefs may influence their views on ethical issues, such as marriage, family, and social justice. Religious practices, such as prayer, fasting, or pilgrimage, may also serve as important expressions of identity.

At the collective level, religion often serves as a unifying force for communities. Shared religious beliefs and practices create bonds of solidarity and belonging among members of the same faith. Religious festivals, rituals, and places of worship provide spaces for communal expression and the reinforcement of collective identity. For example, the celebration of religious holidays, such as Christmas, Eid, or Diwali, often serves as a way for communities to come together and reaffirm their shared values and traditions.

Religion also plays a powerful role in shaping cultural traditions. Many cultural practices—such as marriage ceremonies, funeral rites, and rites of passage—are deeply intertwined with religious beliefs. These traditions serve as markers of identity, connecting individuals to their community and their faith. For many religious communities, these practices are seen as sacred expressions of their beliefs and are passed down from generation to generation as a way of preserving cultural and religious identity.

In addition to shaping personal and collective identity, religion has often been a force for social and political change. Throughout history, religious movements have played a central role in struggles for justice, equality, and human rights. For example, leaders like **Martin Luther King Jr.**, **Mahatma Gandhi**, and **Desmond Tutu** drew on their religious beliefs to advocate for social justice and nonviolent resistance against oppression. At the same time, religion has also been a source of conflict, particularly when different religious groups vie for power or when religious beliefs are used to justify exclusion or violence.

Tradition: The Keeper of Cultural Memory

Tradition refers to the customs, beliefs, and practices that are passed down from generation to generation. These traditions often serve as a way of preserving cultural identity, connecting individuals to their ancestors and providing continuity between the past and the present.

Traditions are often deeply embedded in cultural rituals and ceremonies, which mark important life events and social transitions. **Weddings, birthdays, coming-of-age ceremonies,** and **funerals** are all examples of cultural traditions that play a central role in shaping identity. These rituals are often accompanied by specific practices, such as the wearing of traditional clothing, the preparation of special foods, or the performance of particular dances or songs. Through these practices, individuals reaffirm their connection to their culture and their place within their community.

In many cultures, oral traditions—such as storytelling, songs, and proverbs—serve as a way of transmitting cultural knowledge and values. These stories often carry important moral lessons, historical memories, and spiritual teachings. For example, Indigenous communities around the world often rely on oral traditions to pass down their cultural knowledge, including their understanding of the land, the seasons, and the natural world. These traditions not only preserve cultural memory but also reinforce collective identity by connecting individuals to their ancestors and their cultural heritage.

Tradition is not static; it evolves over time in response to changing social, political, and economic conditions. In many cases, individuals and communities adapt traditional practices to fit contemporary realities, creating new forms of cultural expression. However, the tension between preserving tradition and embracing change is often a source of conflict, particularly in societies undergoing rapid modernization or globalization. In such contexts, the preservation of cultural traditions can become a point of resistance against external pressures to conform to dominant global norms.

The Role of Cultural Exchange in a Globalized World

In today's interconnected world, **cultural exchange** is more prevalent than ever before. Globalization has brought people, goods, ideas, and cultural practices into closer contact, leading to the blending and mixing of cultures on an unprecedented scale. While this exchange can lead to greater understanding and cooperation, it also raises important questions about cultural identity, appropriation, and the power dynamics that shape these exchanges.

The Benefits of Cultural Exchange

Cultural exchange occurs when people from different cultures interact and share their ideas, traditions, and ways of life. This exchange can take many forms, from the spread of music, art, and literature to the adoption of foreign foods, fashion, and technologies. In an increasingly globalized world, cultural exchange is facilitated by migration, travel, trade, and digital communication.

One of the key benefits of cultural exchange is that it fosters **cross-cultural understanding** and **empathy**. When people are exposed to different cultures, they gain new perspectives on life and learn to appreciate the diversity of human experience. For example, studying another culture's history, religion, or artistic traditions can deepen one's understanding of the world and challenge stereotypes or prejudices.

Cultural exchange also encourages **creativity and innovation**. Throughout history, the blending of cultural influences has led to the creation of new art forms, technologies, and social practices. For example, the **Renaissance** in Europe was fueled by the exchange of ideas between European scholars and those of the Islamic world, leading to advancements in science, art, and philosophy.

Similarly, modern popular culture, from music to film, is often the result of the fusion of different cultural influences.

In addition, cultural exchange promotes **economic growth** by facilitating the flow of goods, services, and ideas across borders. Globalization has enabled the spread of cultural products—such as films, books, and music—on a global scale, creating new markets and opportunities for cultural industries. The exchange of culinary traditions, for example, has given rise to the global popularity of cuisines such as sushi, pizza, and curry, enriching people's diets and creating new business opportunities.

The Challenges of Cultural Exchange: Appropriation and Power Imbalances

While cultural exchange can lead to mutual understanding and enrichment, it can also raise challenges related to **cultural appropriation** and **power imbalances**. Cultural appropriation occurs when elements of one culture are taken and used by members of another culture, often without permission or understanding. This can be particularly problematic when the appropriated culture belongs to a historically marginalized or oppressed group.

Cultural appropriation is often criticized because it involves the extraction of cultural elements—such as clothing, hairstyles, or religious symbols—without respect for their cultural significance or the context in which they originated. For example, the commercialization of Indigenous designs or the use of sacred symbols in fashion or entertainment can be seen as disrespectful and harmful to the communities from which these elements are taken. In many cases, cultural appropriation perpetuates power imbalances by allowing dominant groups to profit from the cultural heritage of marginalized groups without giving credit or compensation.

Another challenge of cultural exchange is the risk of **cultural homogenization**. As global cultural products— such as Hollywood films, fast food chains, and Western fashion—become more widespread, there is a concern that local cultures may be eroded or overshadowed by dominant global cultures. This can lead to the loss of cultural diversity and the disappearance of traditional practices, languages, and ways of life.

To address these challenges, it is important to promote **respectful cultural exchange** that values diversity and acknowledges the contributions of all cultures. This involves recognizing the power dynamics that shape cultural exchange and ensuring that marginalized cultures have the opportunity to represent themselves and share their cultural practices on their own terms.

Globalization and the Rise of Hybrid Identities

One of the most significant outcomes of cultural exchange in a globalized world is the rise of **hybrid identities**. As people move across borders and cultures interact, individuals increasingly draw on multiple cultural influences to shape their identities. This blending of cultural elements leads to the creation of new, hybrid forms of identity that reflect the complexity of contemporary life.

For example, many children of immigrants grow up navigating multiple cultural worlds, combining elements of their parents' culture with those of the society in which they are raised. This can result in a hybrid identity that incorporates different languages, traditions, and values. In some cases, hybrid identities are celebrated as a source of creativity and innovation, as individuals blend cultural influences to create new forms of expression. In other cases, hybrid identities can lead to feelings of alienation or tension, as individuals struggle to reconcile conflicting cultural expectations.

Globalization has also given rise to **transnational identities**, where individuals feel connected to multiple countries or regions. For example, members of the **diaspora**—people who live outside their country of origin— often maintain strong ties to their homeland while also integrating into their host society. These transnational identities reflect the fluidity of identity in a globalized world, where people can belong to multiple communities and navigate different cultural contexts.

Conclusion

Culture and identity are deeply intertwined, shaping how individuals and communities understand themselves and relate to the world. Through the exploration of language, religion, and tradition, we see how culture provides the framework for both personal and collective identity, influencing everything from individual behavior to social cohesion. In a globalized world, cultural exchange offers opportunities for creativity, innovation, and mutual understanding, while also presenting challenges related to power dynamics and cultural appropriation.

As we navigate the complexities of the modern world, it is essential to cultivate a deep appreciation for cultural diversity and a critical awareness of how culture shapes our identities. By engaging with different cultures, respecting the traditions and experiences of others, and recognizing the evolving nature of identity, we can foster a more inclusive, empathetic, and interconnected global society. Understanding culture and identity is not just a matter of knowledge; it is a vital tool for building bridges between people, promoting social justice, and enriching the human experience.

Chapter 8: The Psychology of Human Behavior

Understanding human behavior is essential to comprehending the world we live in. Every decision, interaction, and motivation we experience is rooted in the complex workings of the human mind. Psychology, the scientific study of behavior and mental processes, provides valuable insights into why people think, feel, and act the way they do. By exploring key concepts from psychology, we can better understand ourselves, our relationships, and the broader social dynamics that shape human life.

This chapter explores fundamental ideas from psychology that help explain human actions and motivations. We will examine how **cognitive biases** and **social influences** affect decision-making, as well as discuss the significance of **empathy** and **emotional intelligence** in understanding and interacting with others. By developing a deeper understanding of these psychological principles, we can enhance our ability to navigate the complexities of human behavior and improve our interpersonal relationships.

Key Concepts from Psychology That Help Explain Human Actions and Motivations

Human behavior is shaped by a complex interplay of biological, psychological, and environmental factors. Psychology seeks to understand these factors by exploring the underlying mechanisms that drive our actions and motivations. Some of the key concepts in psychology that offer insights into human behavior include **motivation, personality, learning**, and **development**.

Motivation: Why We Do What We Do

Motivation is the driving force behind human behavior. It refers to the processes that initiate, direct, and sustain goal-oriented actions. Motivation can be influenced by both internal factors (such as biological needs, desires, and emotions) and external factors (such as rewards, social pressures, and environmental cues).

There are two primary types of motivation:

- **Intrinsic motivation**: This type of motivation comes from within the individual. People are intrinsically motivated when they engage in an activity for the sake of the activity itself, because it is enjoyable, satisfying, or aligned with their values. For example, a person might be intrinsically motivated to play music because they find it fulfilling or to pursue a hobby because it brings them joy.

- **Extrinsic motivation**: Extrinsic motivation comes from external factors, such as rewards, recognition, or avoiding punishment. People are extrinsically motivated when they perform an activity to achieve an external goal, such as earning money, receiving praise, or meeting societal expectations. For example, a student might study hard to earn a good grade or a worker might strive for a promotion to receive a higher salary.

Psychologists have developed various theories to explain human motivation, including **Maslow's Hierarchy of Needs**. According to Maslow, humans have a set of hierarchical needs that range from basic physiological requirements (such as food and shelter) to more complex psychological needs (such as self-esteem and self-actualization). Maslow's theory suggests that individuals are motivated to fulfill their basic needs before they can focus on higher-level goals like personal growth and self-expression.

Other motivation theories, such as **Self-Determination Theory**, emphasize the importance of autonomy, competence, and relatedness in fostering motivation. According to this theory, people are more motivated when they feel in control of their actions, believe they are capable of achieving their goals, and experience meaningful connections with others.

Understanding motivation is crucial for explaining why people pursue certain goals and make specific decisions. Whether driven by internal desires or external rewards, motivation influences how people approach challenges, overcome obstacles, and pursue their aspirations.

Personality: The Unique Characteristics that Shape Behavior

Personality refers to the enduring patterns of thoughts, feelings, and behaviors that make individuals unique. Personality plays a significant role in shaping how people interact with the world and respond to different situations. Psychologists have developed various models to describe personality, one of the most well-known being the **Big Five Personality Traits**:

1. **Openness to Experience**: This trait reflects a person's willingness to try new things, embrace creativity, and explore unfamiliar ideas. People high in openness tend to be curious, imaginative, and open-minded, while those low in openness may prefer routine and familiarity.

2. **Conscientiousness**: This trait relates to a person's level of organization, dependability, and self-discipline. Highly conscientious individuals are often reliable, goal-oriented, and detail-focused, while those low in conscientiousness may be more spontaneous or disorganized.

3. **Extraversion**: Extraversion describes a person's sociability, energy, and tendency to seek out social interaction. Extraverts are outgoing and enjoy being around others, while introverts tend to be more reserved and may prefer solitary activities.

4. **Agreeableness**: This trait reflects a person's tendency to be compassionate, cooperative, and empathetic. Highly agreeable individuals are often kind, empathetic, and supportive, while those low in agreeableness may be more competitive or self-focused.

5. **Neuroticism**: Neuroticism refers to a person's emotional stability and tendency to experience negative emotions like anxiety, sadness, or anger. People high in neuroticism may be more prone to stress and emotional volatility, while those low in neuroticism tend to be more emotionally stable and resilient.

Personality traits influence how individuals approach different aspects of life, including work, relationships, and decision-making. While personality traits are relatively stable over time, they can be shaped by life experiences, cultural influences, and personal development.

Understanding personality helps explain why people behave differently in similar situations and why some individuals are more inclined toward certain behaviors or reactions. By recognizing the diversity of personalities, we can develop greater empathy and adaptability in our interactions with others.

Learning and Behavior: How We Adapt to Our Environment

Learning is a fundamental process that shapes behavior. Psychologists define **learning** as a relatively permanent change in behavior or knowledge resulting from experience. There are several key theories of learning that help explain how people adapt to their environment:

- **Classical Conditioning**: This theory, developed by **Ivan Pavlov**, explains how individuals learn to associate two stimuli. In Pavlov's famous experiment, he conditioned dogs to salivate when they heard a bell, by repeatedly pairing the bell with the presentation of food. This process of learning by association is known as classical conditioning and explains how certain behaviors, emotions, or reactions can become triggered by specific stimuli.

- **Operant Conditioning**: Developed by **B.F. Skinner**, operant conditioning focuses on how behaviors are influenced by their consequences. According to this theory, behaviors that are followed by positive reinforcement (such as rewards) are more likely to be repeated, while behaviors that are followed by negative reinforcement (such as punishments) are less likely to occur. Operant conditioning is widely used in education, parenting, and behavioral therapy to encourage desired behaviors and discourage unwanted ones.

- **Observational Learning: Albert Bandura's Social Learning Theory** emphasizes the role of observation and imitation in learning. According to Bandura, individuals learn by observing the behaviors of others and the outcomes of those behaviors. For example, a child may learn to share toys by watching a sibling receive praise for doing so. Observational learning highlights the importance of social influence and role models in shaping behavior.

These learning theories illustrate how individuals adapt to their environment by forming associations, responding to rewards and punishments, and modeling their behavior after others. Learning is not only essential for acquiring new skills and knowledge but also for understanding how behaviors are shaped by external factors.

Developmental Psychology: How Behavior Evolves Over Time

Developmental psychology examines how people change and grow over the course of their lives. It explores how cognitive, emotional, and social development unfold from infancy to old age. One of the most influential developmental theories is **Jean Piaget's Theory of Cognitive Development**, which outlines how children's thinking evolves in stages:

1. **Sensorimotor Stage** (birth to 2 years): In this stage, infants learn about the world through their senses and actions. They develop object permanence—the understanding that objects continue to exist even when out of sight.

2. **Preoperational Stage** (2 to 7 years): Children in this stage begin to use language and symbols to represent objects and ideas. However, their thinking is often egocentric, meaning they struggle to see things from other people's perspectives.

3. **Concrete Operational Stage** (7 to 11 years): At this stage, children develop logical thinking and understand concepts like conservation (the idea that quantity remains the same even when the shape or appearance changes).

4. **Formal Operational Stage** (12 years and up): Adolescents and adults in this stage develop the ability to think abstractly, reason logically, and solve complex problems.

Another important developmental theory is **Erik Erikson's Psychosocial Stages of Development**, which emphasizes the impact of social experiences across the lifespan. According to Erikson, individuals go through eight stages of psychosocial development, each characterized by a specific conflict that must be resolved (e.g., trust vs. mistrust, identity vs. role confusion). Successful resolution of these conflicts leads to healthy psychological development, while failure to resolve them can result in challenges later in life.

Understanding developmental psychology helps us appreciate how behavior, thought processes, and emotional responses change over time. It also highlights the importance of early experiences, social interactions, and life transitions in shaping who we become.

How Cognitive Biases and Social Influences Affect Decision-Making

Human decision-making is not always rational. While we may like to think of ourselves as logical beings, our decisions are often influenced by **cognitive biases**— systematic errors in thinking that affect our judgments and perceptions. These biases, along with social influences, can lead to flawed decision-making, misunderstandings, and miscommunication.

Cognitive Biases: The Shortcuts That Distort Our Thinking

Cognitive biases are mental shortcuts, or **heuristics**, that our brains use to simplify complex information processing. While these shortcuts are often useful, they can also lead to errors in judgment. Some of the most common cognitive biases include:

- **Confirmation Bias**: This bias refers to the tendency to seek out, interpret, and remember information that confirms our existing beliefs, while ignoring or dismissing information that contradicts them. For example, if someone believes in a particular political ideology, they may only pay attention to news sources that support their views and ignore evidence that challenges them. Confirmation bias can reinforce stereotypes, perpetuate misinformation, and contribute to polarization.

- **Anchoring Bias**: Anchoring bias occurs when individuals rely too heavily on the first piece of information they receive (the "anchor") when making decisions. For example, if a person is negotiating the price of a car, the initial price offered may serve as an anchor, influencing their perception of what a fair price should be, even if the initial price is arbitrary.

- **Availability Heuristic**: This bias occurs when people make decisions based on how easily they can recall examples from memory. For instance, if a person has recently heard about a plane crash, they may overestimate the likelihood of air travel accidents, even though flying is statistically safer than driving. The availability heuristic can lead to overreactions to rare or sensational events, such as media coverage of natural disasters or crime.

- **Hindsight Bias**: Hindsight bias is the tendency to believe, after an event has occurred, that the outcome was predictable all along. This bias can make people overestimate their ability to predict events and underestimate the role of chance. For example, after a sports team wins a championship, fans might claim they "knew" the team would win, even though the outcome was uncertain.

- **Groupthink**: Groupthink occurs when a group of people prioritizes consensus and cohesion over critical thinking and independent decision-making. In groupthink, individuals may suppress dissenting opinions to avoid conflict, leading to poor decisions. This bias is common in highly cohesive groups, such as corporate boards or political teams, where pressure to conform can stifle creativity and lead to faulty decision-making.

Understanding cognitive biases is essential for improving decision-making. By recognizing these biases, we can take steps to counteract them, such as seeking out diverse perspectives, questioning our assumptions, and being aware of how our emotions influence our choices.

Social Influences: How Others Shape Our Decisions

Human behavior is also heavily influenced by social factors. **Social psychology** examines how individuals are affected by the presence and actions of others, whether in face-to-face interactions or through broader societal norms.

One of the key social influences on decision-making is **conformity**—the tendency to align one's behavior with the norms and expectations of a group. People often conform to fit in with others, avoid conflict, or gain approval. Conformity can be positive, helping individuals adhere to societal rules and cooperate with others. However, it can also lead to problematic behaviors, such as **peer pressure** or the **bystander effect** (where individuals are less likely to help someone in distress if others are present, assuming someone else will intervene).

Another important social influence is **obedience to authority**. Psychologist **Stanley Milgram's famous obedience experiments** demonstrated that people are often willing to follow orders from authority figures, even when those orders conflict with their personal morals. In Milgram's study, participants were instructed to administer electric shocks to another person (who was actually an actor) by an authority figure in a lab coat. Many participants complied with the instructions, even when they believed they were causing harm. This experiment highlighted the powerful role of authority in shaping human behavior, as well as the potential for individuals to act against their own ethical judgments under pressure.

Social norms—the unwritten rules that govern behavior in society—also shape decision-making. Norms influence everything from how people dress and speak to how they behave in public or interact in relationships. People often internalize social norms without being consciously aware of them, and these norms can vary widely across cultures and communities.

Understanding the impact of social influences on behavior can help individuals make more informed decisions and resist pressure to conform or obey when it conflicts with their values. It also highlights the importance of fostering environments that encourage independent thinking and ethical decision-making.

The Importance of Empathy and Emotional Intelligence in Understanding Others

At the heart of human relationships lies the ability to understand and connect with others on an emotional level. **Empathy** and **emotional intelligence** are key components of effective communication, collaboration, and conflict resolution. These skills not only improve our interactions with others but also enhance our capacity to navigate the social and emotional complexities of human life.

Empathy: The Ability to Understand and Share Feelings

Empathy is the capacity to understand and share the feelings of another person. It involves recognizing others' emotions, putting oneself in their shoes, and responding with care and compassion. Empathy is a crucial component of social relationships because it enables individuals to connect with others on a deep emotional level.

There are two main types of empathy:

- **Cognitive empathy**: This refers to the ability to understand what someone else is feeling or thinking. It involves perspective-taking, or imagining how another person sees the world. Cognitive empathy allows individuals to anticipate others' needs, understand their concerns, and respond appropriately.

- **Emotional empathy**: This involves actually feeling the emotions that another person is experiencing. Emotional empathy allows individuals to share in another's joy, sadness, or pain, creating a sense of emotional resonance and connection.

Empathy is essential for building trust, resolving conflicts, and fostering cooperation. In relationships, empathy enables individuals to offer support, validate feelings, and show compassion during difficult times. In broader social contexts, empathy promotes understanding across cultural, political, and ideological divides, helping to reduce prejudice and promote social cohesion.

Empathy can be cultivated through active listening, mindfulness, and open-mindedness. By being fully present in conversations, paying attention to nonverbal cues, and seeking to understand others' experiences without judgment, individuals can strengthen their empathetic abilities.

Emotional Intelligence: Managing Emotions for Better Relationships

Emotional intelligence (EI) refers to the ability to recognize, understand, manage, and influence emotions in oneself and others. It is a key factor in successful social interactions and effective leadership. Emotional intelligence is often broken down into five main components:

1. **Self-awareness**: The ability to recognize and understand one's own emotions and how they affect thoughts and behavior.

2. **Self-regulation**: The ability to manage and control one's emotional responses, especially in challenging situations.

3. **Motivation**: The drive to pursue goals with passion, optimism, and perseverance, even in the face of setbacks.

4. **Empathy**: The ability to understand and respond to the emotional needs of others, as discussed earlier.

5. **Social skills**: The ability to build and maintain positive relationships, communicate effectively, and manage conflicts constructively.

Individuals with high emotional intelligence are better equipped to navigate interpersonal relationships, resolve conflicts, and lead with empathy and understanding. Emotional intelligence is particularly important in leadership roles, as it helps leaders connect with their teams, inspire trust, and foster a positive work environment.

Emotional intelligence can be developed through self-reflection, emotional regulation techniques (such as mindfulness or deep breathing), and practicing empathy in daily interactions. By becoming more aware of their own emotional patterns and learning to respond thoughtfully to the emotions of others, individuals can enhance their emotional intelligence and improve their relationships.

Conclusion

The psychology of human behavior is a vast and complex field that offers valuable insights into why we think, feel, and act the way we do. By exploring key psychological concepts—such as motivation, personality, learning, and development—we gain a deeper understanding of the forces that shape human behavior. Cognitive biases and social influences reveal the ways in which our decisions are often shaped by mental shortcuts and external pressures, while empathy and emotional intelligence provide essential tools for understanding and connecting with others on a deeper level.

In a world characterized by increasing social, cultural, and technological complexity, understanding human behavior is more important than ever. Whether navigating personal relationships, engaging in social or political discourse, or making decisions in professional settings, psychological principles offer valuable frameworks for making sense of human actions and motivations. By cultivating empathy, enhancing emotional intelligence, and recognizing the cognitive and social forces that influence behavior, we can build more meaningful relationships, make more informed decisions, and contribute to a more compassionate and understanding society.

Ultimately, understanding human behavior is not just about gaining knowledge—it is about developing the skills and awareness needed to live a more connected, empathetic, and emotionally intelligent life.

Chapter 9: Technology and Its Impact on Society

Technology has become one of the most influential forces shaping modern life. From the way we communicate and work to how we access information and entertainment, technological advancements have fundamentally transformed society. The rise of the **digital age** has connected billions of people worldwide, revolutionized industries, and altered the fabric of everyday life. At the same time, rapid technological development brings challenges, including ethical dilemmas surrounding **artificial intelligence**, **automation**, and **data privacy**. As we navigate a world increasingly driven by technology, understanding its impact on society becomes essential.

In this chapter, we will explore how technology has reshaped communication, work, and daily life, examine the ethical implications of emerging technologies, and discuss how to address the challenges of living in a tech-driven world. By gaining insight into these dynamics, we can better navigate the opportunities and risks that come with technological progress and make informed decisions about the role technology plays in our lives.

The Rise of the Digital Age and How Technology is Transforming Communication, Work, and Daily Life

The digital revolution has transformed the way people live, work, and interact. Over the past few decades, technology has evolved at an unprecedented rate, driven by innovations in computing, the internet, and mobile devices. This digital shift has not only made information more accessible but has also changed how societies function and how individuals experience the world.

The Transformation of Communication

One of the most significant changes brought about by technology is the transformation of **communication**. The rise of the internet, smartphones, and social media has created a global network of interconnected individuals, enabling instantaneous communication across vast distances. In the pre-digital era, communication was often limited by geography and time. Letters took days or weeks to reach their destination, and phone calls were restricted by physical infrastructure. Today, with the click of a button, people can send messages, make video calls, and share content with anyone around the world in real time.

Social media platforms such as Facebook, Twitter, and Instagram have become central to modern communication, allowing individuals to share thoughts, experiences, and opinions with a global audience. These platforms have revolutionized how people connect, creating new forms of social interaction and giving rise to **online communities** that transcend physical boundaries. Social media has also amplified the speed and reach of information, enabling users to access news and updates as events unfold. This has democratized the flow of information, empowering individuals to become content creators and influencers.

However, the rapid spread of information on social media has also brought challenges. The sheer volume of content available online can make it difficult to discern fact from fiction, leading to the spread of **misinformation** and **disinformation**. Additionally, the addictive nature of social media can contribute to **digital burnout**, where individuals feel overwhelmed by the constant influx of notifications, messages, and updates. The pressure to maintain an online presence, as well as the curated and idealized representations of life often portrayed on social media, can also impact mental health, leading to feelings of anxiety, inadequacy, and isolation.

While digital communication has created opportunities for connection and expression, it has also changed the nature of human interaction. **Face-to-face communication** has been partially replaced by digital interactions, which lack the richness of non-verbal cues such as body language and tone of voice. This shift raises important questions about the quality of human relationships in the digital age and how technology affects our ability to connect meaningfully with others.

The Changing Nature of Work

Technology has also dramatically transformed the **workplace** and the nature of employment. The rise of **automation**, **artificial intelligence**, and **remote work** has reshaped industries and altered the relationship between workers and employers. As businesses adapt to technological advancements, new opportunities have emerged, but so have challenges related to job displacement, inequality, and the future of work.

The adoption of **automation** and **AI** has enabled companies to streamline operations, reduce costs, and increase efficiency. Machines and algorithms can now perform tasks that were once reserved for humans, from manufacturing and data analysis to customer service and logistics. While automation has improved productivity and opened the door to new innovations, it has also led to concerns about **job**

displacement. Workers in industries such as manufacturing, retail, and transportation are at risk of losing their jobs as machines take over routine and repetitive tasks. This raises important questions about how society will address the economic and social consequences of automation and ensure that workers have the skills they need to succeed in an evolving job market.

In parallel, **remote work** has become increasingly common, especially in the wake of the COVID-19 pandemic. Advances in communication technologies, such as video conferencing and cloud computing, have made it possible for employees to work from anywhere with an internet connection. For many workers, remote work offers greater flexibility, work-life balance, and the ability to avoid long commutes. However, it also presents challenges related to **isolation**, **work-life boundaries**, and the loss of informal social interactions that occur in traditional office settings.

The rise of the **gig economy**—fueled by platforms like Uber, Lyft, and TaskRabbit—has also transformed the labor market. These platforms enable workers to take on short-term, flexible jobs, often as independent contractors rather than full-time employees. While the gig economy offers flexibility and autonomy, it also raises concerns about job security, benefits, and workers' rights. Gig workers often lack access to traditional employment benefits such as healthcare, paid leave, and retirement savings, leading to increased economic insecurity for many.

As technology continues to shape the future of work, there is an ongoing debate about how to balance the benefits of innovation with the need to protect workers' rights and ensure equitable access to economic opportunities.

Technology in Daily Life

Beyond work and communication, technology has permeated nearly every aspect of **daily life**. From online shopping and streaming entertainment to smart homes and wearable health devices, technology has made life more convenient and connected. Tasks that once required physical effort—such as going to the store, cooking a meal, or managing finances—can now be done with a few taps on a smartphone.

The rise of **e-commerce** has transformed the way people shop. Online platforms like Amazon, Alibaba, and eBay have made it easier for consumers to access a wide range of products from the comfort of their homes. This shift has had a profound impact on traditional brick-and-mortar retail, leading to the closure of many physical stores and changing the landscape of urban centers.

Technology has also revolutionized **healthcare**, with innovations like telemedicine, wearable fitness trackers, and health apps empowering individuals to take control of their health. These tools allow people to monitor their physical activity, heart rate, sleep patterns, and more, enabling them to make informed decisions about their well-being. Telemedicine, in particular, has expanded access to healthcare by allowing patients to consult with doctors remotely, reducing the need for in-person visits and increasing convenience for those in rural or underserved areas.

While these advancements have made life more convenient, they have also raised concerns about the increasing **dependence on technology**. Many people find themselves spending significant amounts of time on their devices, leading to a phenomenon known as **digital addiction**. This overreliance on technology can interfere with relationships, productivity, and mental health, highlighting the need for balance and mindfulness in the digital age.

The Ethical Implications of Artificial Intelligence, Automation, and Data Privacy

As technology continues to advance, it brings with it ethical dilemmas that must be addressed to ensure that technological progress benefits society as a whole. Some of the most pressing ethical issues involve **artificial intelligence (AI)**, **automation**, and **data privacy**. These technologies hold immense potential to improve lives but also pose risks related to fairness, accountability, and personal freedom.

Artificial Intelligence and Automation: Opportunities and Challenges

Artificial intelligence has become one of the most transformative technologies of the 21st century, with applications in healthcare, finance, transportation, and beyond. AI systems are capable of analyzing large amounts of data, learning from patterns, and making decisions with minimal human intervention. While AI offers many benefits, such as improving healthcare diagnostics and optimizing supply chains, it also raises important ethical questions about autonomy, bias, and accountability.

One of the key concerns about AI is the potential for **algorithmic bias**. AI systems are often trained on large datasets, and if these datasets contain biased or incomplete information, the AI system may reproduce or even amplify existing biases. For example, facial recognition technology has been found to have higher error rates when identifying people of color, leading to concerns about racial discrimination in law enforcement and surveillance. Similarly, AI systems used in hiring processes may inadvertently favor candidates who resemble those already in the workforce, perpetuating gender or racial inequalities.

Another ethical concern is the **autonomy** of AI systems. As AI becomes more sophisticated, it may begin to make decisions that have significant consequences for individuals and society. For example, autonomous vehicles may need to make life-or-death decisions in the event of an accident, raising questions about how such decisions should be programmed and who is responsible for the outcomes. The development of **military AI** also raises concerns about the use of autonomous weapons systems and the potential for machines to make decisions about life and death in combat situations.

The rise of **automation** also presents ethical challenges related to **job displacement** and economic inequality. As machines take over routine tasks, many workers may find themselves displaced from their jobs, particularly in industries like manufacturing and retail. While automation has the potential to create new jobs in emerging fields, there is concern that the benefits of automation may not be evenly distributed, leading to greater economic inequality. Policymakers and businesses must grapple with how to balance the need for innovation with the protection of workers and the promotion of economic security.

Data Privacy: Protecting Personal Information in a Digital World

In the digital age, **data** has become one of the most valuable commodities. From social media platforms and search engines to smart devices and e-commerce websites, companies collect vast amounts of personal data about users' behaviors, preferences, and interactions. While this data is often used to improve services and target advertisements, it also raises serious concerns about **privacy** and **surveillance**.

One of the most significant issues related to data privacy is the lack of **transparency** about how personal data is collected, stored, and used. Many individuals are unaware of the extent to which their data is being collected or how it is being shared with third parties. This has led to growing concerns about the erosion of personal privacy and the potential for misuse of sensitive information.

Data breaches have become increasingly common, with high-profile cases involving the theft of personal information from millions of users. These breaches can have serious consequences, including identity theft, financial loss, and reputational damage. As more aspects of life move online, the security of personal data becomes paramount.

Another major concern is the rise of **surveillance capitalism**, a term coined by scholar **Shoshana Zuboff** to describe the business model in which companies collect and monetize personal data. Social media platforms, search engines, and other online services offer free access to users in exchange for collecting data about their online behaviors, which is then sold to advertisers. While this model has enabled the rapid growth of tech companies, it has also led to concerns about the commodification of personal information and the impact on individual autonomy.

Governments also play a role in data privacy, with **mass surveillance** programs raising concerns about civil liberties. In the name of national security, many governments have expanded their surveillance capabilities, collecting vast amounts of data about citizens' online activities. The balance between security and privacy remains a contentious issue, as citizens seek to protect their personal freedoms while governments aim to prevent crime and terrorism.

To address these concerns, policymakers have introduced **data protection regulations**, such as the **General Data Protection Regulation (GDPR)** in the European Union, which sets strict guidelines for how companies collect and process personal data. These regulations are a step toward greater accountability and transparency, but the rapid pace of technological change means that data privacy will continue to be an evolving challenge.

How to Navigate the Challenges of Living in a Tech-Driven World

As technology continues to shape every aspect of life, individuals must develop strategies for navigating the challenges of a tech-driven world. From managing the impact of digital communication on relationships to protecting personal privacy online, there are several key considerations for living well in the digital age.

Digital Well-Being: Balancing Technology Use and Mental Health

One of the most significant challenges of living in a tech-driven world is maintaining a healthy balance between technology use and mental well-being. While technology offers many conveniences and opportunities for connection, it can also contribute to **stress**, **anxiety**, and **digital overload**.

Screen time has become a growing concern, particularly for children and adolescents. Excessive use of smartphones, social media, and video games can interfere with sleep, physical activity, and face-to-face interactions, leading to a range of physical and mental health issues. For adults, the constant presence of work emails, notifications, and social media updates can create a sense of being "always on," making it difficult to disconnect and relax.

To maintain digital well-being, it is important to set **boundaries** around technology use. This might involve establishing **tech-free zones** in the home, such as the bedroom or dining room, to encourage in-person interactions and reduce screen time. Additionally, practicing **mindfulness** around technology use—such as being intentional about when and how we use our devices—can help prevent digital burnout and promote a healthier relationship with technology.

Navigating the Online Information Landscape

In the age of the internet, access to information has never been easier. However, the abundance of online content has also made it more difficult to distinguish between credible sources and misinformation. Navigating the online information landscape requires a critical approach to consuming news and media.

One key strategy is to practice **media literacy**, which involves critically evaluating the sources of information, checking for bias, and verifying facts. This is particularly important in the context of social media, where misinformation can spread rapidly and contribute to the formation of echo chambers, where individuals are only exposed to information that reinforces their existing beliefs.

In addition to being critical consumers of information, individuals should also be aware of the **algorithms** that shape their online experiences. Social media platforms, search engines, and news aggregators use algorithms to prioritize certain content based on user behavior. These algorithms can create **filter bubbles**, where users are only exposed to content that aligns with their preferences, limiting their exposure to diverse perspectives. Being aware of how algorithms influence the content we see online can help us seek out a broader range of viewpoints and engage with information more thoughtfully.

Protecting Privacy and Security Online

In a world where personal data is constantly being collected and shared, individuals must take steps to protect their privacy and security online. While it is difficult to avoid all forms of data collection, there are several strategies for minimizing risk.

One key step is to use **strong, unique passwords** for online accounts and enable **two-factor authentication** whenever possible. This adds an extra layer of security by requiring users to verify their identity using a second method, such as a text message or authentication app.

It is also important to be cautious about the information we share online, particularly on social media. Limiting the amount of personal information shared in public profiles, being mindful of location-sharing features, and regularly reviewing privacy settings can help protect against potential data breaches or misuse of personal information.

Additionally, using tools like **virtual private networks (VPNs)** can help protect online activity from being tracked by third parties, while **ad blockers** and **anti-tracking software** can limit the amount of data collected by websites and advertisers.

Conclusion

Technology is undeniably transforming society in profound ways, from how we communicate and work to how we access information and make decisions. As we navigate the opportunities and challenges of the digital age, it is essential to develop a deeper understanding of the ethical implications of emerging technologies, such as artificial intelligence, automation, and data privacy. These technologies hold immense potential to improve lives, but they also raise important questions about fairness, accountability, and individual autonomy.

Living well in a tech-driven world requires a thoughtful approach to technology use, including maintaining digital well-being, practicing critical media literacy, and protecting privacy and security online. By taking proactive steps to manage our relationship with technology, we can harness its benefits while mitigating its risks.

Ultimately, technology is a tool—how we use it will determine its impact on society. As individuals, communities, and policymakers, we must strive to create a future where technology serves the common good, promotes inclusivity, and enhances the quality of life for all.

Chapter 10: The Environment and Global Sustainability

The environment is the foundation upon which all human life depends. From the air we breathe to the water we drink, the soil that sustains our crops, and the ecosystems that support countless species, the natural world is deeply interconnected with human survival. However, in recent decades, the balance between human activity and the environment has been disrupted, leading to critical challenges that threaten both the planet's health and the long-term well-being of human societies.

Environmental conservatism offers an approach to addressing these challenges by emphasizing responsible stewardship of natural resources and promoting practices that balance the needs of the environment with economic growth and human progress. This chapter explores **the interconnectedness of environmental systems** and human survival, the challenges of **environmental conservatism, resource depletion, and sustainability**, and discusses how both individuals and governments can work toward the **conservation** of the environment.

The Interconnectedness of Environmental Systems and Human Survival

The natural world is composed of complex systems— forests, oceans, rivers, and the atmosphere—that interact with each other in ways that sustain life on Earth. These **environmental systems** provide essential services, such as regulating the climate, purifying air and water, recycling nutrients, and maintaining biodiversity. Human survival is intimately tied to the health of these systems, yet human activity has increasingly disrupted their balance.

Ecosystems and Biodiversity

Ecosystems are communities of living organisms interacting with their physical environment, forming intricate webs of life that support not only the species within them but also the broader environment. **Biodiversity,** or the variety of life within ecosystems, is a key indicator of the health of these systems. High biodiversity ensures that ecosystems are resilient, able to recover from disturbances, and capable of adapting to changing conditions. Healthy ecosystems provide services like pollination, water filtration, and pest control, which are essential to human life.

However, human activities such as deforestation, industrial agriculture, urbanization, and pollution have contributed to a rapid decline in biodiversity. The destruction of habitats leads to species extinction, which weakens ecosystems and reduces their ability to provide these crucial services. The loss of pollinators, for example, directly impacts food production, while the degradation of wetlands compromises water filtration and increases the risk of flooding.

The conservation of biodiversity is not just an environmental issue; it is a human survival issue. Maintaining healthy ecosystems ensures that we continue to benefit from the services they provide. The principles of **environmental conservatism** emphasize the need to manage natural resources responsibly, recognizing that human well-being is inextricably linked to the health of the natural world.

Resource Cycles and Environmental Systems

Environmental systems operate through natural cycles—such as the **carbon, water, and nitrogen cycles**—which regulate the flow of nutrients and energy through the environment. These cycles maintain the balance that sustains life on Earth, recycling essential elements and supporting the growth of plants, animals, and microorganisms.

The **water cycle**, for example, moves water through the atmosphere, land, and oceans, supporting agriculture, human consumption, and natural ecosystems. Disruptions to the water cycle, caused by overuse of freshwater resources, deforestation, and pollution, lead to water shortages, soil degradation, and reduced agricultural productivity. Similarly, the **carbon cycle**, which regulates the amount of carbon dioxide in the atmosphere, is essential for maintaining the Earth's temperature and supporting plant growth. Excessive carbon emissions, driven by industrial activity and deforestation, upset this balance, contributing to rising global temperatures and extreme weather events.

Environmental conservatism calls for the careful management of these natural cycles. By reducing pollution, managing resources sustainably, and protecting natural habitats, we can ensure that these cycles continue to function effectively, supporting both human life and the broader environment.

The Human-Nature Relationship

Humans are not separate from nature; we are part of a dynamic and interconnected web of life. For millennia, human societies have relied on the environment for food, water, shelter, and energy. Our economies, industries, and cultures are built on the resources provided by the natural world. However, as human populations have grown and industrialization has accelerated, the pressure on natural resources has intensified.

The challenge we face today is how to balance the needs of a growing global population with the finite resources of the Earth. This requires a shift in thinking—a recognition that human progress and environmental health are not mutually exclusive, but rather deeply intertwined. Environmental conservatism advocates for a balanced approach, where economic development is pursued in harmony with the protection and preservation of natural resources.

The Challenges of Environmental Conservatism, Resource Depletion, and Sustainability

The concept of environmental conservatism centers on the idea of preserving natural resources and ecosystems for future generations. However, achieving this balance is fraught with challenges, particularly in the face of resource depletion, unsustainable consumption patterns, and the environmental impact of industrialization.

Resource Depletion and Overconsumption

One of the most pressing environmental challenges is **resource depletion**, which occurs when natural resources are consumed at a faster rate than they can be replenished. This is particularly concerning for non-renewable resources, such as fossil fuels, minerals, and metals, which are finite and will eventually run out if current consumption trends continue.

Fossil fuels, such as coal, oil, and natural gas, have powered industrialization and economic growth for over a century.

However, the extraction and burning of fossil fuels have led to environmental degradation, air pollution, and the disruption of natural systems. In addition, as fossil fuel reserves become more difficult to access, the environmental and economic costs of extraction increase, leading to further depletion of ecosystems and resources.

Water scarcity is another critical issue, especially in regions where freshwater resources are already under strain. Agriculture, industry, and urban development place enormous demands on water supplies, and over-extraction of groundwater has led to the depletion of aquifers in many parts of the world. Without sustainable water management practices, this vital resource may become increasingly scarce, with devastating consequences for food security, human health, and ecosystems.

Deforestation and the loss of arable land due to unsustainable farming practices further contribute to resource depletion. Forests, which act as carbon sinks, regulate water cycles, and provide habitats for countless species, are being cleared at alarming rates to make way for agriculture, logging, and urban expansion. This not only reduces biodiversity but also diminishes the planet's ability to regulate carbon dioxide and maintain ecological balance.

Environmental conservatism advocates for the responsible use of resources to prevent depletion and ensure that future generations have access to the same natural wealth that sustains current societies. This requires a shift toward more **sustainable consumption patterns**, where resources are used efficiently, waste is minimized, and renewable resources are prioritized over non-renewable ones.

Sustainability: Meeting Present and Future Needs

Sustainability is at the heart of environmental conservatism. It refers to the ability to meet the needs of the present without compromising the ability of future generations to meet their own needs. However, achieving sustainability is a complex challenge, as it involves balancing economic growth, environmental protection, and social equity.

One of the key obstacles to sustainability is the **unsustainable consumption** of natural resources. In high-income countries, consumption levels far exceed what is necessary to meet basic needs, while in many low-income countries, poverty and lack of access to resources drive environmental degradation. This imbalance creates a global challenge, as the overconsumption of resources in some regions contributes to environmental problems that affect the entire planet, from deforestation and pollution to declining biodiversity and resource depletion.

Another challenge is the **industrial impact** on the environment. The modern economy is heavily dependent on resource-intensive industries such as agriculture, energy production, and manufacturing. These industries are responsible for significant environmental degradation, including deforestation, air and water pollution, and the depletion of natural habitats. Transitioning to more sustainable industries and technologies will be crucial in addressing these environmental challenges.

However, the transition to sustainability also presents economic and political challenges. Many industries and governments are resistant to change, particularly when it involves significant short-term costs or disruptions to established ways of doing business. Environmental conservatism advocates for **innovative solutions** that balance economic growth with environmental stewardship, encouraging industries to adopt sustainable practices and governments to implement policies that promote long-term environmental health.

How Individuals and Governments Can Work Toward Environmental Conservation

Achieving global sustainability requires action at all levels, from individual behaviors to international policies. Both individuals and governments have a crucial role to play in promoting environmental conservation and ensuring that natural resources are used responsibly and equitably.

The Role of Individuals in Environmental Conservation

While governments and industries have significant influence over environmental policies and practices, individual actions also matter. By making conscious choices in everyday life, individuals can contribute to environmental conservation and sustainability.

1. **Reducing Waste:** One of the simplest ways individuals can contribute to environmental conservation is by reducing waste. This includes minimizing the use of single-use plastics, recycling materials whenever possible, and composting organic waste. By reducing the amount of waste that ends up in landfills or pollutes natural ecosystems, individuals can help reduce the environmental impact of consumption.

2. **Sustainable Consumption**: Individuals can also make more sustainable choices by prioritizing

products that are produced using environmentally friendly methods. This might involve choosing locally sourced, organic foods, purchasing products made from renewable materials, or supporting companies that prioritize sustainability in their business practices.

3. **Energy Efficiency:** Reducing energy consumption is another important way individuals can contribute to environmental conservation. Simple actions, such as using energy-efficient appliances, switching to renewable energy sources like solar or wind power, and reducing unnecessary energy use, can have a significant impact on reducing carbon emissions and conserving natural resources.

4. **Supporting Environmental Initiatives:** Individuals can also get involved in local or global environmental initiatives, whether through volunteering for conservation projects, participating in community clean-up efforts, or supporting organizations that advocate for environmental protection. By raising awareness and advocating for change, individuals can help influence broader societal and policy changes.

The Role of Governments in Environmental Conservation

While individual actions are important, governments play a critical role in creating the policy frameworks and regulatory environments necessary to promote **environmental sustainability** on a larger scale. Governments have the power to implement laws and policies that incentivize sustainable practices, protect natural resources, and promote conservation efforts.

1. **Regulating Resource Use:** One of the primary responsibilities of governments is to regulate the use of natural resources. This includes establishing laws that limit deforestation, overfishing, and the extraction of fossil fuels, as well as protecting endangered species and critical habitats. By setting limits on resource use and enforcing environmental regulations, governments can help prevent the over-exploitation of natural resources and promote more sustainable practices.

2. **Promoting Renewable Energy:** Transitioning to renewable energy sources is one of the most important steps governments can take toward environmental sustainability. By investing in renewable energy infrastructure, providing subsidies for clean energy technologies, and setting targets for reducing reliance on fossil fuels, governments can accelerate the shift toward a low-carbon economy. Additionally, public investment in research and development can spur innovation in areas such as energy efficiency, battery storage, and carbon capture technologies.

3. **Implementing Environmental Policies:** Governments can also promote environmental conservation through policies that encourage sustainable agriculture, reduce pollution, and support conservation efforts. For example, policies that promote organic farming and regenerative agriculture can help reduce the environmental impact of food production, while policies that regulate

industrial emissions can improve air and water quality.

4. **Supporting International Cooperation:** Many environmental challenges, such as deforestation, resource depletion, and pollution, are global in scope and require international cooperation to address effectively. Governments must work together through international agreements and treaties to coordinate efforts to protect the environment. Collaborative initiatives, such as protecting the world's oceans, preserving rainforests, and combating desertification, require global partnerships to be effective.

5. **Environmental Education and Public Awareness:** Governments can play a key role in raising public awareness about environmental issues and promoting education on sustainability. Environmental education programs can help individuals understand the importance of conservation and equip them with the knowledge and skills needed to take action. Public campaigns can also encourage citizens to adopt more sustainable lifestyles and support policies that prioritize environmental health.

Conclusion

The environment is not just a backdrop to human life—it is the foundation upon which all human activities depend. The interconnectedness of natural systems and human survival makes it clear that environmental health is essential for human well-being. However, the challenges of resource depletion, environmental degradation, and sustainability require urgent action.

Environmental conservatism offers a framework for addressing these challenges, emphasizing responsible stewardship of natural resources and the need for sustainable practices that balance economic growth with environmental protection. By reducing waste, conserving resources, promoting renewable energy, and supporting international cooperation, individuals and governments can work together to build a more sustainable future.

Ultimately, the responsibility for environmental conservation lies with all of us. By making conscious choices in our daily lives, advocating for sustainable policies, and supporting conservation efforts, we can ensure that future generations inherit a world that is as rich in natural resources and biodiversity as the one we live in today. Environmental sustainability is not just a matter of protecting nature—it is about securing the future of humanity itself.

Chapter 11: Global Health and Wellness

Health is fundamental to the well-being of individuals and societies, influencing every aspect of human life. The health of populations, often measured through public health systems, plays a key role in determining a nation's social and economic stability. In today's interconnected world, where diseases and health challenges cross borders, global health has emerged as one of the most critical areas of concern. Issues such as pandemics, malnutrition, mental health crises, and unequal access to healthcare present significant challenges, requiring coordinated efforts from governments, international organizations, and individuals to ensure the health and well-being of all people.

This chapter explores the **importance of public health systems** and how they function, examines **major global health challenges** like pandemics, malnutrition, and mental health crises, and discusses the crucial role of **health literacy** in improving individual and collective well-being. By understanding these issues, we can gain insight into how global health systems work, what obstacles they face, and how we can contribute to improving health outcomes worldwide.

The Importance of Public Health Systems and How They Function

Public health is concerned with the prevention of disease, the promotion of health, and the protection of populations from health threats. Unlike individual healthcare, which focuses on treating illness in specific patients, public health aims to improve the health of entire communities by addressing the social, environmental, and economic factors that influence health outcomes. Strong public health systems are essential for managing large-scale health challenges, such as infectious disease outbreaks, environmental hazards, and chronic diseases.

What is Public Health?

Public health is a multidisciplinary field that draws on science, policy, and community engagement to promote health and prevent disease. It encompasses a wide range of activities, from immunization programs and health education campaigns to disease surveillance and emergency preparedness. Public health professionals work to identify and mitigate health risks at the population level, aiming to improve overall health outcomes and reduce health disparities.

The **core functions of public health** include:

1. **Assessment**: Public health systems monitor and assess the health needs of communities, collecting data on disease prevalence, risk factors, and health behaviors. This information is essential for identifying emerging health threats and shaping public health policies.

2. **Policy Development**: Based on health assessments, public health officials develop policies and programs aimed at preventing disease and promoting health. These policies may involve regulations, such as smoking bans or food safety standards, as well as public health campaigns to encourage healthy behaviors, such as vaccination or exercise.

3. **Assurance**: Public health systems are responsible for ensuring that healthcare services are accessible and

of high quality. This includes overseeing healthcare providers, regulating healthcare facilities, and addressing gaps in care, especially for vulnerable populations.

4. **Prevention and Control**: A primary focus of public health is preventing the spread of infectious diseases through vaccination programs, hygiene initiatives, and health education. Public health systems also work to control non-communicable diseases, such as heart disease and diabetes, by promoting healthy lifestyles and managing risk factors like tobacco use and poor diet.

5. **Emergency Response**: Public health systems play a critical role in responding to health emergencies, such as pandemics, natural disasters, or bioterrorism. This involves coordinating resources, providing medical care, and communicating with the public to mitigate the impact of the crisis.

How Public Health Systems Function

Public health systems operate at multiple levels, from local health departments to international organizations. These systems are typically composed of **government agencies, non-governmental organizations (NGOs), healthcare providers**, and **academic institutions**. Collaboration between these entities is essential for addressing complex health challenges that affect large populations.

At the national level, public health is typically managed by government agencies, such as the **Centers for Disease Control and Prevention (CDC)** in the United States or **Public Health England** in the UK. These agencies are responsible for implementing national health policies, monitoring health trends, and coordinating responses to health emergencies.

At the international level, organizations like the **World Health Organization (WHO)** play a key role in coordinating global health efforts. The WHO works with governments, NGOs, and the private sector to address global health threats, such as infectious diseases, environmental health risks, and non-communicable diseases. In addition to providing technical expertise and setting health standards, the WHO facilitates international collaboration and resource sharing during health crises.

Public health systems also rely on **community health workers** and **local health departments** to provide care and education at the grassroots level. These workers play a critical role in promoting health in underserved communities, conducting health screenings, distributing vaccines, and providing information on disease prevention. By engaging with communities directly, local public health workers help build trust and ensure that public health initiatives reach the people who need them most.

The Role of Prevention in Public Health

Prevention is the cornerstone of public health. Rather than focusing solely on treating diseases after they occur, public health systems aim to prevent illness before it happens. **Primary prevention** involves addressing the root causes of disease, such as promoting healthy behaviors and reducing exposure to environmental hazards. Examples of primary prevention include anti-smoking campaigns, vaccination programs, and efforts to improve access to clean water and sanitation.

Secondary prevention focuses on early detection and treatment of diseases, with the goal of preventing more serious health outcomes. This includes screening programs for diseases like cancer or diabetes, which can help identify health problems early, when they are more easily treated.

Tertiary prevention aims to improve the quality of life for individuals who are already affected by chronic diseases or disabilities. This may involve providing rehabilitation services, managing long-term conditions, or supporting patients with ongoing medical care.

By focusing on prevention, public health systems can reduce the burden of disease, improve quality of life, and lower healthcare costs. For example, vaccination programs have successfully eliminated or controlled many infectious diseases, such as smallpox and polio, saving millions of lives worldwide.

Major Global Health Challenges: Pandemics, Malnutrition, and Mental Health Crises

Global health is shaped by a wide range of challenges that impact populations in different regions and socioeconomic contexts. Some of the most pressing global health challenges today include pandemics, malnutrition, and mental health crises. These issues are complex, interconnected, and require coordinated efforts from public health systems, governments, and international organizations to address effectively.

Pandemics: Preparing for and Responding to Global Health Emergencies

Pandemics are global outbreaks of infectious diseases that spread rapidly across countries and continents, affecting large populations. The COVID-19 pandemic, which began in 2019, is a stark reminder of how quickly infectious diseases can disrupt societies, overwhelm healthcare systems, and cause widespread illness and death. Pandemics pose a unique challenge to global health because they transcend national borders, requiring coordinated international responses to contain and mitigate their impact.

One of the key lessons from the COVID-19 pandemic is the importance of **pandemic preparedness**. Public health systems must be equipped to detect and respond to emerging infectious diseases before they become widespread. This requires robust disease surveillance systems, early warning mechanisms, and rapid response teams that can deploy resources and interventions in affected areas.

Vaccination is one of the most effective tools for preventing the spread of infectious diseases. During the COVID-19 pandemic, the development and distribution of vaccines were crucial for controlling the virus and reducing its impact on populations. However, vaccine distribution is often unequal, with low- and middle-income countries facing significant barriers to accessing vaccines and other medical supplies. Addressing these inequities is essential for ensuring that all populations are protected from the threat of pandemics.

In addition to vaccines, public health systems must be prepared to implement **non-pharmaceutical interventions (NPIs)**, such as social distancing, mask-wearing, and quarantine measures, to slow the spread of disease. Public communication is also critical during pandemics, as clear and accurate information helps build public trust and compliance with health guidelines.

The global nature of pandemics highlights the need for international cooperation in managing health emergencies. Organizations like the **World Health Organization (WHO)** play a central role in coordinating global responses, sharing data, and providing technical support to countries in need. Multilateral efforts, such as the **COVAX initiative**, aim to ensure equitable access to vaccines and treatments for all countries, regardless of their economic status.

Malnutrition: Addressing Hunger and Food Insecurity

Malnutrition is a widespread global health challenge that affects millions of people, particularly in low- and middle-income countries. **Malnutrition** occurs when individuals do not receive the necessary nutrients to maintain good health, either due to a lack of food (undernutrition) or an overconsumption of unhealthy foods (overnutrition). Both forms of malnutrition have serious consequences for health, development, and well-being.

Undernutrition is most prevalent in regions facing food insecurity, where access to adequate food is limited by poverty, conflict, or environmental factors such as drought and crop failure. Undernutrition is particularly dangerous for children, as it can lead to **stunted growth**, weakened immune systems, and increased vulnerability to infections. According to the **World Food Programme (WFP)**, more than 820 million people worldwide suffer from hunger, and malnutrition is responsible for nearly half of all deaths among children under the age of five.

Efforts to combat malnutrition must address the root causes of hunger, including poverty, inequality, and inadequate access to food and clean water. **Agricultural development** plays a key role in improving food security, as investments in sustainable farming practices can increase food production and improve nutrition in vulnerable communities. In addition, **food aid programs** and **nutrition interventions**, such as providing fortified foods and supplements, are critical for addressing acute malnutrition in crisis situations.

Overnutrition is another major global health issue, particularly in high-income countries and rapidly developing regions. Overnutrition is characterized by the overconsumption of calories, often in the form of highly processed, unhealthy foods that are high in sugar, fat, and salt. This can lead to obesity, diabetes, heart disease, and other chronic health conditions. The global rise in obesity, particularly among children, is a growing concern, as it places a heavy burden on healthcare systems and contributes to the global epidemic of non-communicable diseases.

Addressing malnutrition requires a comprehensive approach that includes improving food access, promoting healthy diets, and supporting policies that encourage the production and consumption of nutritious foods. Public health campaigns aimed at reducing the consumption of sugary drinks and processed foods, as well as efforts to promote **breastfeeding** and child nutrition, are essential for tackling both undernutrition and overnutrition.

Mental Health: The Silent Global Health Crisis

Mental health is an often-overlooked aspect of global health, yet it is a critical component of overall well-being. **Mental**

health disorders—such as depression, anxiety, and substance abuse—affect millions of people worldwide, with significant consequences for individuals, families, and societies. The **World Health Organization (WHO)** estimates that over 450 million people live with mental health conditions, making mental health disorders one of the leading causes of disability globally.

The stigma surrounding mental health remains a major barrier to care, preventing many individuals from seeking help or receiving the treatment they need. In many countries, mental health services are underfunded, and access to care is limited, particularly in low- and middle-income regions. The **mental health treatment gap**—the difference between the number of people who need care and those who receive it—is substantial, with many individuals unable to access affordable or culturally appropriate mental health services.

The **COVID-19 pandemic** has exacerbated the global mental health crisis, as prolonged social isolation, economic uncertainty, and fear of illness have led to increased rates of anxiety, depression, and stress-related disorders. The pandemic has highlighted the need for robust mental health support systems that can respond to the emotional and psychological needs of populations during times of crisis.

Addressing mental health requires a comprehensive approach that includes **early intervention**, **community-based care**, and the integration of mental health services into primary healthcare systems. Public health campaigns aimed at raising awareness of mental health issues, reducing stigma, and promoting help-seeking behaviors are critical for improving mental health outcomes. Additionally, governments and international organizations must invest in mental health services and ensure that mental health is treated with the same urgency as physical health.

The Role of Health Literacy in Improving Individual and Collective Well-Being

Health literacy is the ability to obtain, process, and understand basic health information and services needed to make informed health decisions. **Health literacy** is essential for improving both individual and collective well-being, as it empowers people to take control of their health, make informed choices, and navigate the complexities of the healthcare system.

What is Health Literacy?

Health literacy involves more than just the ability to read and understand health information—it encompasses a range of skills, including the ability to communicate with healthcare providers, interpret medical instructions, and evaluate the credibility of health information. Individuals with high health literacy are better equipped to manage their health, prevent disease, and adhere to treatment plans, while those with low health literacy may struggle to understand medical advice, leading to poorer health outcomes.

For example, a person with high health literacy might be able to read a prescription label, understand the recommended dosage, and follow the instructions correctly. They may also be able to evaluate whether a health article they read online is based on credible evidence or whether it contains misinformation. In contrast, a person with low health literacy may have difficulty understanding basic medical terminology, leading to confusion about their diagnosis or treatment options.

Health literacy is influenced by a variety of factors, including **education level**, **language proficiency**, and **access to health information**. Vulnerable populations, such as the elderly, non-native speakers, and those with lower levels of education, are more likely to experience low health literacy. This can create barriers to accessing healthcare, understanding health risks, and engaging in preventive behaviors.

The Importance of Health Literacy in Public Health

Improving health literacy is a key goal of public health systems, as it has a direct impact on health outcomes and healthcare costs. When individuals have the knowledge and skills needed to make informed health decisions, they are more likely to engage in **preventive health behaviors**, such as getting vaccinated, practicing good hygiene, and adopting a healthy lifestyle. This, in turn, reduces the burden of disease and lowers healthcare costs by preventing avoidable illnesses and hospitalizations.

Health literacy is also critical for navigating **complex health systems**. In many countries, healthcare systems can be difficult to navigate, with multiple providers, insurance options, and treatment plans to choose from. Individuals with high health literacy are better able to understand their rights as patients, access the care they need, and advocate for themselves in healthcare settings.

At the community level, improving health literacy can help address **health disparities** by ensuring that all individuals have the information they need to make informed choices about their health. Public health campaigns that provide clear, culturally appropriate information about disease prevention, healthy behaviors, and access to care can help reduce health inequalities and improve outcomes for marginalized populations.

Strategies for Improving Health Literacy

Improving health literacy requires a multifaceted approach that involves healthcare providers, educators, governments, and communities. Some key strategies for improving health literacy include:

1. **Clear communication**: Healthcare providers can improve health literacy by using plain language when explaining medical information, avoiding jargon, and providing written materials that are easy to understand. Visual aids, such as diagrams or videos, can also help patients better understand complex health concepts.

2. **Health education**: Schools and community organizations can play a key role in promoting health literacy by providing education on topics such as nutrition, exercise, mental health, and disease prevention. Early health education helps individuals develop the skills and knowledge they need to make informed health decisions throughout their lives.

3. **Culturally sensitive materials**: Public health campaigns should be designed with cultural sensitivity in mind, taking into account the language, beliefs, and values of different populations. Providing health information in multiple languages and using culturally relevant examples can help ensure that all individuals have access to the information they need.

4. **Digital health literacy**: In today's digital age, health information is increasingly found online. However, not all information on the internet is accurate or trustworthy. Improving **digital health literacy** involves teaching individuals how to evaluate the credibility of online health resources, understand the risks of misinformation, and use technology to manage their health effectively.

By improving health literacy, we can empower individuals to take control of their health, reduce health disparities, and promote better health outcomes for all.

Conclusion

Global health and wellness are critical components of a thriving society, and public health systems play a vital role in ensuring that populations are protected from disease, malnutrition, and other health threats. As we face global challenges such as pandemics, malnutrition, and mental health crises, it is essential to strengthen public health systems, improve access to healthcare, and promote health literacy at all levels of society.

By understanding how public health systems function, recognizing the major health challenges facing the world, and supporting efforts to improve health literacy, we can work together to create a healthier, more equitable world for all people. Public health is not just the responsibility of governments and healthcare providers—it is a collective effort that requires the participation of individuals, communities, and nations to ensure that everyone has the opportunity to lead a healthy, fulfilling life.

Chapter 12: Religion, Spirituality, and Philosophies of Life

Throughout human history, religion, spirituality, and philosophical beliefs have played an integral role in shaping cultures, societies, and individual lives. These belief systems provide frameworks for understanding existence, morality, ethics, and the mysteries of life. They offer meaning and purpose, guiding how people live, think, and relate to the world and each other. From ancient traditions to modern secular philosophies, human beings have sought answers to life's fundamental questions through diverse spiritual practices and belief systems.

This chapter explores the world's major religions and spiritual practices, examines how belief systems shape **moral values, ethics, and worldviews**, and delves into the complex relationship between **religion and society**. By understanding these aspects, we can gain a deeper appreciation of the role that religion and spirituality play in the human experience and how they continue to influence our global society today.

An Exploration of the World's Major Religions and Spiritual Practices

Religion and spirituality have taken many forms throughout history, reflecting the diversity of human cultures and experiences. While religious traditions vary widely, they often address common themes such as the nature of the divine, the meaning of life, the problem of suffering, and the path to salvation or enlightenment. In this section, we will explore some of the world's major religions and spiritual practices, focusing on their core beliefs and teachings.

Hinduism

Hinduism is one of the world's oldest and most complex religions, with roots in the Indian subcontinent that stretch back more than 4,000 years. Hinduism is a pluralistic and diverse tradition, with no single founder, central authority, or unified set of beliefs. It encompasses a wide range of practices, philosophies, and texts, and it allows for a great degree of personal interpretation.

At the heart of Hinduism is the belief in **Brahman**, the ultimate, formless reality that pervades the universe. Brahman is both immanent and transcendent, manifesting in countless forms and deities. Hindus may worship many gods and goddesses, including **Vishnu**, **Shiva**, **Lakshmi**, and **Durga**, each representing different aspects of the divine. Hinduism also teaches the doctrine of **karma** (the law of cause and effect) and **reincarnation**, the belief that the soul is reborn in different forms until it achieves **moksha**, or liberation from the cycle of birth and death.

Hindu practice is centered on **dharma**, or righteous living, which involves fulfilling one's duties to family, society, and the cosmos. **Yoga** and **meditation** are common spiritual practices that aim to unite the individual soul with the divine. The sacred texts of Hinduism include the **Vedas**, the **Upanishads**, and the **Bhagavad Gita**, which provide philosophical guidance and spiritual wisdom.

Buddhism

Buddhism, founded by **Siddhartha Gautama** (the Buddha) in the 5th century BCE, is a spiritual tradition focused on understanding the nature of suffering and the path to liberation. Like Hinduism, Buddhism originated in India, but it spread across Asia and developed into various schools, including **Theravada**, **Mahayana**, and **Vajrayana**.

Central to Buddhism is the **Four Noble Truths**, which diagnose the problem of suffering (dukkha) and offer a solution. According to the Buddha, suffering arises from **desire and attachment**, and the cessation of suffering is possible through the **Eightfold Path**, a guide to ethical living, mental discipline, and wisdom. The ultimate goal of Buddhism is to achieve **nirvana**, a state of liberation from suffering, ignorance, and the cycle of rebirth (samsara).

Buddhist practice includes **meditation**, **mindfulness**, and **ethical conduct** (such as nonviolence and compassion). Monasticism plays a central role in many Buddhist traditions, with monks and nuns dedicating their lives to spiritual practice and teaching. The **Tripitaka** (or Pali Canon) is the authoritative text in Theravada Buddhism, while Mahayana Buddhism includes additional scriptures such as the **Lotus Sutra** and the **Heart Sutra**.

Christianity

Christianity is the world's largest religion, with more than 2 billion followers. It is based on the life, teachings, death, and resurrection of **Jesus Christ**, whom Christians believe to be the **Son of God** and the **Savior** of humanity. Christianity teaches that through Jesus' sacrificial death, humans are offered salvation from sin and eternal life with God.

The central beliefs of Christianity are outlined in the **Nicene Creed**, which affirms the doctrine of the **Trinity**: one God in three persons—Father, Son, and Holy Spirit. The core message of Christianity is the **gospel**, or "good news," that through faith in Jesus Christ, individuals can be reconciled with God and experience eternal life.

Christianity is divided into three major branches: **Roman Catholicism**, **Eastern Orthodoxy**, and **Protestantism**. Each branch has its own traditions, rituals, and interpretations of Christian doctrine. The **Bible**, composed of the **Old Testament** and the **New Testament**, is the sacred text of Christianity, providing moral and spiritual guidance to believers.

Christian practices include **prayer**, **worship**, and participation in the **sacraments** (such as baptism and communion). Christians gather for communal worship in churches, and many denominations place a strong emphasis on missionary work, spreading the message of Jesus' love and salvation.

Islam

Islam, the world's second-largest religion, was founded in the 7th century CE by the Prophet **Muhammad**, who Muslims believe to be the final prophet in a long line of messengers sent by God (Allah). Islam teaches the belief in **one God (Allah)**, who is all-powerful, merciful, and compassionate. The teachings of Islam are contained in the **Qur'an**, the holy book revealed to Muhammad, which Muslims regard as the literal word of God.

The core beliefs of Islam are outlined in the **Five Pillars**:

1. **Shahada** (faith): The declaration that there is no god but Allah, and Muhammad is His prophet.

2. **Salat** (prayer): Muslims are required to pray five times a day facing Mecca.

3. **Zakat** (charity): Muslims are required to give a portion of their wealth to help those in need.

4. **Sawm** (fasting): During the month of **Ramadan**, Muslims fast from dawn until sunset to develop self-discipline and empathy for the less fortunate.

5. **Hajj** (pilgrimage): Muslims who are able are required to make a pilgrimage to Mecca at least once in their lifetime.

Islam is divided into two main branches: **Sunni** and **Shia**, which differ primarily in their views on the rightful leadership of the Muslim community after Muhammad's death. Islamic law, or **Sharia**, provides guidance on all aspects of life, from personal conduct to social and legal matters. Central to Islam is the concept of **submission to the will of Allah**, with the aim of living a life that reflects justice, compassion, and mercy.

Judaism

Judaism is one of the world's oldest monotheistic religions, with a history that spans more than 3,000 years. The Jewish faith is based on the belief in one God (Yahweh) and the covenant between God and the Jewish people, who are considered the "chosen people" to live according to God's laws and serve as a light to the nations. The sacred texts of Judaism include the **Torah**, which contains the law (or commandments), and the **Tanakh** (Hebrew Bible), which includes writings on history, prophecy, and wisdom.

Judaism places a strong emphasis on **ethical conduct**, **social justice**, and **community life**. The observance of the **Sabbath** (a day of rest), **festivals** (such as **Passover** and **Yom Kippur**), and dietary laws (kashrut) are central to

Jewish religious practice. Jewish worship takes place in synagogues, and spiritual leadership is provided by **rabbis**, who guide the community in the study of scripture and the application of Jewish law.

Judaism has three major branches: **Orthodox, Conservative**, and **Reform**. These branches differ in their interpretations of Jewish law and tradition, with Orthodox Judaism maintaining the strictest adherence to traditional practices, while Conservative and Reform movements embrace more modern and flexible approaches to Jewish life.

Spirituality and New Age Movements

In addition to organized religions, there has been a growing interest in **spirituality** and **New Age movements**, particularly in the West. These movements emphasize personal spiritual growth, self-awareness, and connection with the divine, often drawing on elements from multiple religious traditions, including Buddhism, Hinduism, and indigenous practices.

Spirituality, as distinct from religion, is often understood as a more individualized and experiential approach to the sacred. For many, it involves exploring inner consciousness, cultivating mindfulness, and seeking a direct connection with the divine or the universe. Practices such as **meditation, yoga**, and **energy healing** (such as **Reiki**) are common in contemporary spiritual movements.

New Age spirituality often promotes ideas of **holistic wellness, environmental sustainability**, and the belief in universal interconnectedness. It encourages individuals to find their own path to spiritual fulfillment, often rejecting dogma and institutionalized religion in favor of personal experience and intuition.

How Belief Systems Shape Moral Values, Ethics, and Worldviews

Religions and spiritual traditions offer more than just explanations for the mysteries of existence—they also provide ethical frameworks that guide how people live their lives, make decisions, and interact with others. These belief systems shape **moral values**, define what is right and wrong, and influence broader worldviews on issues such as justice, human rights, and the meaning of life.

Morality and Ethics in Religion

Most religious traditions provide ethical guidelines for living a good and moral life. These guidelines are often based on sacred texts, teachings from religious leaders, or the example of religious figures (such as Jesus in Christianity, the Buddha in Buddhism, or Muhammad in Islam). Religious ethics typically emphasize values such as compassion, honesty, humility, and love for others.

For example, in Christianity, the **Golden Rule**—"Do unto others as you would have them do unto you"—encapsulates the ethical principle of treating others with kindness and respect. In Buddhism, the principle of **right action**, part of the Eightfold Path, encourages individuals to act in ways that do not harm others and that promote peace and well-being. In Islam, the concept of **justice** (adl) and the responsibility to care for the less fortunate are central ethical teachings.

In addition to these universal values, religious ethics often address specific issues such as charity, the sanctity of life, sexual morality, and the treatment of animals and the environment. Religious ethics may also provide guidance on how to resolve conflicts, promote forgiveness, and seek reconciliation.

Philosophical and Secular Ethics

Beyond religious ethics, many people turn to **philosophical** and **secular** ethical systems to guide their moral decision-making. These systems often focus on reasoning, logic, and human experience to determine what is right and just. Philosophical ethics can be divided into several major schools of thought, including **utilitarianism, deontology,** and **virtue ethics**.

- **Utilitarianism**: This ethical theory, associated with philosophers **Jeremy Bentham** and **John Stuart Mill**, holds that the right course of action is the one that maximizes overall happiness or well-being. In other words, the ethical choice is the one that produces the greatest good for the greatest number of people.

- **Deontology**: Developed by **Immanuel Kant**, deontological ethics is based on the idea that certain actions are morally required, regardless of their consequences. Kant argued that individuals have a duty to act in accordance with moral principles, such as honesty and fairness, because these principles are inherently right.

- **Virtue Ethics**: Rooted in the work of **Aristotle**, virtue ethics emphasizes the development of good character traits (virtues) such as courage, temperance, and wisdom. According to this view, ethical behavior arises from cultivating virtuous habits and striving to become a morally excellent person.

Secular ethics also includes contemporary movements such as **humanism**, which emphasizes human rights, social justice, and the dignity of individuals. Humanism seeks to promote a moral framework based on reason, empathy, and a commitment to the well-being of all people, without reference to religious doctrine.

How Belief Systems Shape Worldviews

Belief systems—whether religious, spiritual, or philosophical—profoundly shape individuals' worldviews, or the fundamental ways in which they understand the nature of reality, humanity's place in the universe, and the purpose of life. Worldviews influence how people interpret events, make decisions, and engage with social, political, and environmental issues.

For example, a **Christian worldview** may include beliefs in the existence of a loving God, the inherent worth of every person, and the importance of salvation and eternal life. This worldview can influence attitudes toward social justice, charity, and human rights, as well as personal values such as humility, forgiveness, and compassion.

A **Buddhist worldview**, on the other hand, may emphasize the impermanence of all things, the interconnectedness of life, and the importance of reducing suffering through mindfulness and compassion. This worldview may shape attitudes toward nonviolence, environmental conservation, and the practice of meditation as a means of personal and spiritual growth.

In a **secular worldview**, individuals may reject the existence of a higher power and instead focus on human reason, scientific inquiry, and ethical principles grounded in shared human values. Secular worldviews often emphasize individual autonomy, social progress, and the pursuit of knowledge as key components of a meaningful life.

Worldviews are not static; they evolve in response to personal experiences, cultural influences, and historical events. In an increasingly globalized world, many individuals draw on multiple belief systems—religious, spiritual, and secular—to form their worldview, creating complex and dynamic perspectives on life.

The Relationship Between Religion and Society

Religion has long been intertwined with society, shaping cultural norms, social structures, political systems, and legal frameworks. The relationship between religion and society is complex and multifaceted, involving both cooperation and conflict. In this section, we will explore how religion influences society, the role of religion in governance and law, and the challenges and opportunities posed by religious pluralism.

Religion and Cultural Identity

Religion plays a significant role in shaping cultural identity and social cohesion. For many communities, religious traditions, rituals, and holidays are central to their sense of identity and belonging. Religious festivals, such as **Christmas**, **Diwali**, **Ramadan**, and **Passover**, bring people together to celebrate shared beliefs and values, fostering a sense of unity and continuity with the past.

Religious institutions, such as churches, temples, mosques, and synagogues, often serve as community centers, providing not only spiritual guidance but also social support, education, and charitable services. Religious leaders, such as **priests**, **imams**, and **rabbis**, play an important role in guiding their communities and providing moral and ethical leadership.

In many cultures, religious symbols, art, and architecture are central to the expression of cultural identity. For example, the **Hindu temples of India**, the **cathedrals of Europe**, and the **mosques of the Islamic world** are not only places of worship but also expressions of cultural heritage and artistic achievement.

Religion, Politics, and Law

The relationship between religion and politics has been a source of both cooperation and tension throughout history. In many societies, religion has played a central role in shaping laws, governance, and political institutions. For example, in medieval Europe, the **Catholic Church** wielded significant political power, influencing monarchs and shaping the legal and social order. In Islamic societies, **Sharia law** has historically guided both religious and political life, providing a comprehensive framework for governance and justice.

In modern times, the relationship between religion and politics varies widely across different countries and cultures. In some nations, religion continues to play a significant role in governance, while in others, there is a clear separation between church and state. For example, in **Saudi Arabia**, Islamic law is the foundation of the legal system, while in countries like **France** and the **United States**, secularism is enshrined in the constitution, and religion is kept separate from government affairs.

The question of how religion should influence politics and law remains a contentious issue in many parts of the world. Some argue that religious values are essential for promoting moral governance and social cohesion, while others believe that religion should be kept out of politics to ensure the protection of individual rights and freedoms.

Religious Pluralism and Tolerance

In an increasingly interconnected world, religious pluralism—the coexistence of multiple religious traditions within a society—has become a defining feature of modern life. Religious pluralism presents both opportunities and challenges for societies seeking to promote harmony, tolerance, and mutual understanding among diverse communities.

Religious pluralism allows individuals to encounter different belief systems, learn from one another, and find common ground in shared values such as compassion, justice, and respect for human dignity. Interfaith dialogue, for example, provides a platform for people of different religions to engage in meaningful conversations about their beliefs and work together on issues such as poverty, peace, and environmental sustainability.

However, religious pluralism can also lead to tensions, particularly when religious groups feel that their beliefs or practices are threatened by secularization or other religious traditions. Religious conflicts, both historical and contemporary, often arise from struggles over power, identity, and cultural dominance. Promoting **religious tolerance** and understanding is essential for building inclusive societies where people of all faiths (and none) can coexist peacefully.

Secularization and the Future of Religion

In many parts of the world, particularly in Europe and North America, there has been a trend toward **secularization**—the decline of religious influence in public life and the rise of secular worldviews. This trend has been driven by factors such as scientific advancements, modernization, and the increasing separation of religion from politics and education. Secularization has led to a decline in religious affiliation and participation in many countries, as well as the growth of **agnosticism** and **atheism**.

Despite this trend, religion continues to play a significant role in many societies, particularly in regions such as **Africa**, **Asia**, and the **Middle East**, where religious practice remains a central part of daily life. Moreover, new religious movements, spiritual practices, and interfaith initiatives continue to emerge, demonstrating that religion and spirituality are evolving in response to the challenges and opportunities of the modern world.

The future of religion is likely to be shaped by ongoing changes in society, including globalization, migration, technological advancements, and social movements. As religious communities adapt to these changes, they will continue to play a vital role in shaping culture, ethics, and the human search for meaning.

Conclusion

Religion, spirituality, and philosophical belief systems have been central to human life for millennia, shaping cultures, moral values, and worldviews. They provide answers to life's fundamental questions, guide ethical behavior, and offer frameworks for understanding the mysteries of existence. Whether through the teachings of major world religions, the practices of spiritual seekers, or the reasoning of secular philosophers, these belief systems continue to influence how individuals and societies navigate the complexities of life.

Understanding the diversity of religious and spiritual traditions, as well as the role of belief systems in shaping morality and social norms, is essential for appreciating the richness of human culture and the ongoing search for meaning. As the world becomes increasingly interconnected, fostering mutual respect, tolerance, and dialogue between different belief systems will be crucial for building a more inclusive and harmonious global society.

Ultimately, religion and spirituality are not just about doctrine or ritual—they are about the human quest for purpose, connection, and understanding in an ever-changing world. By exploring these belief systems with an open mind, we can deepen our understanding of ourselves, others, and the world we share.

Chapter 13: Conflict and Cooperation in a Globalized World

In an increasingly interconnected world, the dynamics of **conflict and cooperation** play a significant role in shaping global affairs. While globalization has brought nations closer together through trade, technology, and cultural exchange, it has also heightened tensions between countries, ethnic groups, and political factions. Issues such as war, terrorism, and geopolitical rivalry continue to pose serious threats to global stability, while international cooperation through diplomacy, peacekeeping, and organizations like the United Nations offers hope for addressing common challenges such as poverty, security, and human rights violations.

This chapter will explore the **causes of global conflict**, including war, terrorism, and geopolitical tensions; examine the **importance of diplomacy, international organizations, and peacekeeping efforts**; and discuss how **global cooperation** can be a powerful tool for addressing some of the most pressing issues of our time, such as poverty, climate change, and human rights.

The Causes of Global Conflict: War, Terrorism, and Geopolitical Tensions

Conflict has been a constant in human history, driven by a variety of factors including political ambition, economic competition, religious and ethnic divisions, and the pursuit of power. Despite efforts to promote peace and cooperation, conflict continues to erupt in many parts of the world. Understanding the underlying causes of conflict is crucial for addressing its root causes and preventing future violence.

War and Armed Conflict

War remains one of the most destructive forms of conflict, often resulting in widespread death, displacement, and economic devastation. Wars can be caused by a multitude of factors, including territorial disputes, competition for resources, political ideology, and the desire for power and dominance. **Interstate wars**, where two or more nations engage in armed conflict, have become less common in recent decades, but **civil wars** and **intrastate conflicts**—often driven by internal divisions within a country—continue to rage in many regions, particularly in parts of Africa, the Middle East, and Southeast Asia.

One of the primary causes of war is **nationalism**, or the desire of a group to assert its identity and independence. Nationalism has historically led to both the formation of new states and violent conflicts, as groups seek autonomy or resist foreign control. **Ethnic and religious divisions** can exacerbate these tensions, especially when different groups are vying for political power, resources, or recognition.

Economic inequality and competition for **natural resources** are also major drivers of conflict. In regions where valuable resources such as oil, minerals, or water are scarce or unevenly distributed, competition for control over these assets can fuel violence. In addition, global trade dynamics, foreign intervention, and the extraction of resources by multinational corporations often intensify local conflicts, as marginalized populations fight for their livelihoods and access to resources.

The breakdown of governance and the absence of strong political institutions can further contribute to conflict, creating **failed states** where armed groups, warlords, and criminal networks operate with impunity. In such situations, violence can spiral out of control, leading to prolonged wars and humanitarian crises.

Terrorism and Asymmetric Conflict

Terrorism is a form of conflict that involves the use of violence and intimidation by non-state actors to achieve political, religious, or ideological objectives. Unlike traditional warfare, terrorism often targets civilians, creating a climate of fear and uncertainty. Terrorist groups use asymmetric tactics, meaning they operate with limited resources and against much stronger state actors, often relying on guerrilla warfare, suicide bombings, and cyber-attacks.

The motivations behind terrorism vary, but many terrorist groups emerge in response to **political grievances**, **perceived injustices**, or **foreign occupation**. Religious extremism has played a prominent role in modern terrorism, with groups such as **Al-Qaeda** and the so-called **Islamic State (ISIS)** using radical interpretations of Islam to justify acts of violence against perceived enemies. However, terrorism is not limited to religious motivations; far-right extremism, separatist movements, and political ideologies such as anarchism and communism have also led to acts of terror.

Terrorism is particularly challenging for governments to address because it is difficult to combat using conventional military strategies. Terrorist groups often operate covertly and exploit weak or failed states where law enforcement is ineffective. Moreover, the use of counterterrorism measures, such as military interventions or surveillance, can sometimes backfire, leading to further radicalization and resentment among local populations.

Geopolitical Tensions and the Struggle for Power

Geopolitical tensions arise from the strategic rivalry between nations as they seek to expand their influence and protect their national interests. The **Cold War** between the United States and the Soviet Union was a prime example of how competing geopolitical ideologies—**capitalism** versus **communism**—can drive conflict, leading to proxy wars, arms races, and diplomatic standoffs. Although the Cold War ended in the early 1990s, geopolitical rivalries continue to shape the global order.

In recent years, the rise of **China** as a global power, the resurgence of **Russia** under President Vladimir Putin, and the relative decline of American hegemony have created a multipolar world in which multiple countries vie for dominance. These shifts in global power dynamics have led to conflicts in regions such as the **South China Sea**, **Eastern Europe**, and the **Middle East**, where major powers assert their influence through economic, military, and diplomatic means.

Economic competition is another source of geopolitical tension, as nations seek to secure access to resources, markets, and technological advantages. The trade wars between the United States and China, for example, have raised concerns about the potential for economic rivalry to escalate into military conflict. Additionally, the **control of strategic resources**, such as oil, natural gas, and rare earth minerals, often leads to disputes between nations, with energy security being a key driver of both cooperation and conflict.

Geopolitical tensions can also be fueled by historical grievances, territorial disputes, and competing national identities. In regions such as **Kashmir**, the **Korean Peninsula**, and the **Israel-Palestine conflict**, longstanding territorial and ethnic disputes continue to stoke tensions between neighboring countries, making the prospects for peace elusive.

The Importance of Diplomacy, International Organizations, and Peacekeeping Efforts

While conflict remains a persistent feature of the international system, diplomacy and international cooperation offer powerful tools for preventing and resolving disputes. **Diplomacy, international organizations**, and **peacekeeping efforts** are essential for maintaining global peace and security, promoting human rights, and addressing the root causes of conflict.

Diplomacy: Negotiation and Conflict Resolution

Diplomacy is the practice of conducting negotiations between nations to resolve disputes, build alliances, and promote cooperation. Diplomats work to prevent conflicts through dialogue and compromise, often mediating between conflicting parties to find peaceful solutions. **Preventive diplomacy** involves identifying and addressing potential conflicts before they escalate into violence, while **crisis diplomacy** seeks to de-escalate tensions during periods of conflict.

One of the key tools of diplomacy is **negotiation**, in which representatives of different countries come together to discuss their interests and seek mutually acceptable solutions. **Summit meetings, bilateral talks,** and **multilateral forums** provide opportunities for leaders to engage in direct dialogue, build trust, and reduce misunderstandings. **Track II diplomacy,** which involves unofficial negotiations by non-state actors such as academics, NGOs, or religious leaders, can also complement official diplomatic efforts by fostering communication and understanding between conflicting parties.

Mediation and **arbitration** are also important diplomatic tools for resolving disputes. In mediation, a neutral third party assists in facilitating negotiations and helping conflicting parties reach an agreement. In arbitration, an impartial body makes a binding decision on a dispute based on international law or agreed-upon principles.

The success of diplomacy depends on the willingness of conflicting parties to compromise and the skill of negotiators in finding common ground. While diplomacy does not always prevent conflict, it remains the most effective means of managing international relations and reducing the likelihood of war.

International Organizations: Promoting Peace and Security

International organizations play a critical role in promoting global peace and security by providing forums for cooperation, establishing norms and rules, and coordinating responses to crises. The **United Nations (UN)** is the foremost international organization dedicated to maintaining peace, protecting human rights, and promoting development. Founded in 1945 after the devastation of World War II, the UN has been at the center of global efforts to prevent conflict and foster cooperation among nations.

The **UN Security Council**, composed of five permanent members (the United States, Russia, China, France, and the United Kingdom) and ten rotating members, is responsible for addressing threats to international peace and security. The Security Council has the authority to impose **sanctions**, authorize **peacekeeping missions**, and, in some cases, approve the use of military force to maintain peace. While the Security Council plays a key role in conflict resolution, its effectiveness is sometimes limited by the **veto power** of its permanent members, who may block resolutions that conflict with their national interests.

Other UN agencies, such as the **World Health Organization (WHO)**, the **United Nations Development Programme (UNDP)**, and the **United Nations High Commissioner for Refugees (UNHCR)**, contribute to global stability by addressing issues such as health, poverty, and humanitarian crises. These agencies work in cooperation with governments and non-governmental organizations (NGOs) to provide assistance to vulnerable populations, rebuild conflict-affected areas, and promote sustainable development.

In addition to the UN, regional organizations such as the **European Union (EU)**, the **African Union (AU)**, and the **Association of Southeast Asian Nations (ASEAN)** play important roles in conflict prevention and resolution. These organizations promote regional stability by facilitating dialogue, providing economic assistance, and supporting peacebuilding efforts.

Peacekeeping: Stabilizing Conflict Zones

One of the most visible forms of international cooperation in conflict resolution is **peacekeeping**, in which international forces are deployed to conflict zones to maintain order, protect civilians, and support the implementation of peace agreements. UN **peacekeeping missions** have been instrumental in stabilizing war-torn regions, preventing the resurgence of violence, and facilitating the transition to peace.

Peacekeeping operations typically involve the deployment of **military personnel**, **police forces**, and **civilian experts** to monitor ceasefires, protect vulnerable populations, and assist in the reconstruction of institutions. Peacekeepers are often tasked with disarming combatants, overseeing elections, and supporting the establishment of legal and political institutions in post-conflict societies.

While peacekeeping has been successful in preventing the escalation of conflicts in many cases, it also faces significant challenges. Peacekeeping missions are often underfunded and lack sufficient resources to fully address the complexities of the conflicts they are tasked with managing. Additionally, peacekeepers may be deployed in situations where there is no clear peace to keep, making their work difficult and dangerous.

Despite these challenges, peacekeeping remains an essential tool for maintaining global stability and protecting civilians in conflict zones. As conflicts become more complex and protracted, there is a growing need for innovative approaches to peacekeeping that address the root causes of conflict and promote long-term peacebuilding.

How Global Cooperation Can Address Pressing Issues: Poverty, Security, and Human Rights

In a globalized world, the challenges we face—whether related to conflict, poverty, security, or human rights—are interconnected and require cooperative solutions. No single nation can effectively address these issues alone. Instead, global cooperation through international organizations, multilateral agreements, and collective action is essential for creating a more just and stable world.

Addressing Poverty and Inequality

Poverty and **inequality** are major drivers of conflict and instability, as they exacerbate social tensions, fuel grievances, and undermine political legitimacy. Addressing poverty is not only a moral imperative but also a strategic necessity for promoting global peace and security.

Global cooperation is critical in the fight against poverty, as economic disparities often transcend national borders. Organizations such as the **World Bank**, the **International Monetary Fund (IMF)**, and the **United Nations Development Programme (UNDP)** work with governments to provide financial assistance, promote economic reforms, and implement development projects aimed at reducing poverty and inequality.

Foreign aid plays an important role in supporting development in low-income countries, particularly in areas such as healthcare, education, infrastructure, and agriculture. In addition to aid, **fair trade** and **debt relief** initiatives can help create more equitable economic opportunities for developing nations, reducing the structural barriers that contribute to poverty.

However, poverty reduction efforts must be accompanied by policies that promote **inclusive growth**, protect vulnerable populations, and address systemic inequalities. Global cooperation can help ensure that the benefits of economic development are shared more equitably, reducing the risk of conflict and promoting long-term stability.

Global Security: Combating Terrorism and Cybersecurity Threats

In an interconnected world, security threats—such as **terrorism, organized crime**, and **cybersecurity** risks—are increasingly transnational in nature, requiring coordinated responses from the global community. **International cooperation** is essential for combating these threats, as no single nation has the capacity to address them alone.

The **Global Counterterrorism Forum (GCTF)**, the **Financial Action Task Force (FATF)**, and the **International Criminal Police Organization (INTERPOL)** are examples of international organizations that facilitate cooperation in the fight against terrorism and transnational crime. These organizations help countries share intelligence, coordinate law enforcement efforts, and disrupt the financing of terrorist networks.

In the realm of **cybersecurity**, global cooperation is critical for addressing the growing threat of cyberattacks on critical infrastructure, financial systems, and government institutions. Cyberattacks can have devastating consequences for national security, economic stability, and public trust in government. International agreements on cybersecurity standards, information sharing, and cyber defense strategies are essential for protecting against these threats.

At the same time, global security efforts must be balanced with respect for human rights and civil liberties. Counterterrorism measures, such as mass surveillance, military interventions, and extrajudicial actions, can sometimes lead to abuses and exacerbate the very problems they are intended to address. A **human rights-based approach** to security—one that respects the dignity and rights of all individuals—is essential for building trust and legitimacy in global security efforts.

Promoting Human Rights and Social Justice

Human rights are fundamental to global peace and security. Violations of human rights—whether through authoritarian regimes, ethnic cleansing, gender discrimination, or exploitation—often lead to conflict, instability, and humanitarian crises. Global cooperation is essential for protecting human rights and promoting social justice around the world.

The **Universal Declaration of Human Rights**, adopted by the United Nations in 1948, sets out a common standard of human rights for all people, regardless of nationality, race, gender, or religion. International human rights organizations, such as **Amnesty International** and **Human Rights Watch**, work to monitor human rights abuses and advocate for the protection of vulnerable populations.

The **International Criminal Court (ICC)** plays a key role in holding individuals accountable for crimes against humanity, war crimes, and genocide. The ICC prosecutes those responsible for the most serious human rights violations, providing a mechanism for justice and accountability when national legal systems fail to act.

In addition to legal mechanisms, global cooperation is needed to address the root causes of human rights violations, such as poverty, inequality, and discrimination. Efforts to promote **gender equality**, protect **migrant rights**, and combat **racial and ethnic discrimination** are critical for building inclusive societies where the rights of all individuals are respected and protected.

Conclusion

In a globalized world, conflict and cooperation are two sides of the same coin. While the causes of conflict—whether war, terrorism, or geopolitical rivalry—continue to pose significant challenges, the mechanisms of diplomacy, international organizations, and peacekeeping efforts provide hope for resolving disputes and promoting global peace. At the same time, global cooperation is essential for addressing the pressing issues of poverty, security, and human rights that affect the well-being of individuals and societies.

By understanding the complex dynamics of conflict and cooperation, we can better appreciate the interconnectedness of global challenges and the need for collective action. Whether through diplomatic negotiations, international treaties, or grassroots movements for social justice, cooperation remains the most powerful tool for creating a more peaceful, equitable, and sustainable world.

In the end, global peace and stability depend on the ability of nations, communities, and individuals to work together in pursuit of shared goals. As we face the challenges of the 21st century, the choice between conflict and cooperation will define the future of our world. By choosing cooperation, we can build a future where peace, justice, and human dignity are realized for all.

Chapter 14: The Role of Art, Music, and Literature

Art, music, and literature are fundamental forms of human expression that transcend the boundaries of time, culture, and geography. Throughout history, they have served as mirrors reflecting the human condition, shaping the societies they arise from and influencing the course of history. These creative mediums offer insights into the emotions, thoughts, and experiences of individuals and communities, enabling us to understand the world from diverse perspectives. In the process, they shape cultural identities, fuel social movements, and deepen our connection to humanity.

In this chapter, we will explore how **creative expressions reflect and shape society**, discuss the role of **art, music, and literature in cultural identity and social movements**, and examine how appreciating the arts can provide a window into different perspectives and experiences, enhancing our understanding of the world.

How Creative Expressions Reflect and Shape Society

Art, music, and literature are both products of society and agents of change within it. They are born out of the cultural, political, and social context of their time and, in turn, can influence the values, beliefs, and actions of individuals and groups. By reflecting on the human experience, creative expressions allow us to explore complex themes such as identity, power, beauty, injustice, love, and suffering.

Art as a Reflection of Society

Art has always been a reflection of the societies from which it emerges, serving as a visual record of cultural, political, and historical developments. From ancient cave paintings to modern digital installations, art provides a means of interpreting the world and exploring what it means to be human.

In many cases, art has served as a way to depict the social realities of the time, whether through glorifying political leaders, capturing religious narratives, or portraying the struggles of marginalized communities. **Renaissance art**, for example, reflected the rediscovery of classical ideals of beauty and the human form, while celebrating religious themes and the growing influence of the Church. The detailed representations of the human body in works like **Michelangelo's David** and **Leonardo da Vinci's Vitruvian Man** symbolize the Renaissance belief in human potential and the divine in humanity.

Similarly, art can serve as a critique of society, challenging the status quo and offering new ways of seeing the world. In the 19th century, movements like **Realism** and **Impressionism** sought to depict the everyday lives of ordinary people, rejecting the idealized forms and heroic subject matter of earlier academic art. Artists like **Gustave Courbet** and **Édouard Manet** captured scenes of working-class life, urban poverty, and social inequality, highlighting the challenges faced by the lower classes in industrialized societies.

In the 20th century, **modern art movements** such as **Cubism**, **Dadaism**, and **Surrealism** reacted against traditional forms of representation, seeking to break down established conventions and push the boundaries of artistic expression. These movements were often deeply influenced by the social and political upheavals of the time, including World War I, the rise of totalitarian regimes, and the rapid pace of industrialization and technological change. Artists like **Pablo Picasso**, **Marcel Duchamp**, and **Salvador Dalí** used their work to challenge societal norms, question reality, and express the disillusionment of a world in crisis.

Today, contemporary art continues to reflect society, often addressing pressing issues such as climate change, migration, identity politics, and globalization. Through various forms of media, including painting, sculpture, photography, performance, and digital art, artists engage with their audiences in dialogues about the world around them. **Street art** and **public installations**, for example, have become powerful tools for activism and social commentary, giving voice to marginalized communities and raising awareness of issues like racial injustice, environmental degradation, and political corruption.

Music as a Reflection of Society

Music has long been a means of expressing collective experiences, emotions, and ideas, reflecting the cultural, social, and political landscape of its time. Whether through folk songs, classical compositions, or contemporary pop, music can capture the spirit of an era and serve as a powerful tool for communication and connection.

In traditional societies, music often played a central role in rituals, ceremonies, and communal gatherings, serving both sacred and secular purposes. In ancient Greece, for instance, music was seen as essential to the education of citizens, believed to have the power to shape character and morality.

Greek tragedies were often accompanied by choruses and musical interludes, emphasizing the emotional weight of the story and the moral lessons to be learned.

Over time, music became a reflection of the social and political changes taking place in different regions of the world. **Baroque** and **Classical music**, for example, were closely tied to the courts of European monarchs, reflecting the grandeur and order of the aristocratic class. Composers like **Johann Sebastian Bach**, **Wolfgang Amadeus Mozart**, and **Ludwig van Beethoven** composed music that embodied the ideals of the Enlightenment, emphasizing balance, reason, and human emotion.

In the 20th century, **jazz**, **blues**, and **rock and roll** emerged as musical genres that reflected the experiences of African American communities in the United States, capturing both the pain of racial injustice and the joy of resilience and cultural expression. Musicians like **Louis Armstrong**, **Billie Holiday**, and **Chuck Berry** broke new ground by blending traditional African rhythms with Western musical structures, creating a distinctly American sound that would influence music worldwide.

During the 1960s and 1970s, **protest music** became a powerful force for social change, reflecting the growing dissatisfaction with the Vietnam War, racial inequality, and other social issues. Artists like **Bob Dylan**, **Joan Baez**, and **John Lennon** used their music to advocate for peace, justice, and civil rights, providing a soundtrack to the social movements of the era. Songs like Dylan's "Blowin' in the Wind" and Lennon's "Imagine" became anthems of protest, inspiring generations of activists and ordinary people to envision a better world.

Today, music continues to reflect the social and political concerns of the global community. Genres like **hip-hop**, **reggae**, and **world music** serve as platforms for expressing cultural identity, resistance, and solidarity. Artists like **Kendrick Lamar**, **Beyoncé**, and **Burna Boy** address issues of racism, inequality, and empowerment through their music, reaching audiences across the world and sparking conversations about justice and change.

Literature as a Reflection of Society

Literature has the unique ability to delve into the complexities of human experience, offering both a reflection of society and a vehicle for exploring its deeper truths. Whether through fiction, poetry, drama, or nonfiction, literature allows writers to engage with the political, social, and cultural issues of their time, providing readers with insights into the human condition.

In many cases, literature serves as a **chronicle of history**, capturing the major events and ideas that shape societies. For example, **Homer's epics**, the **Iliad** and the **Odyssey**, provide a window into the values and beliefs of ancient Greek society, exploring themes such as honor, fate, and the consequences of war. Similarly, **Shakespeare's plays**, such as **Hamlet** and **Macbeth**, delve into questions of power, ambition, morality, and the human struggle for meaning in a chaotic world.

In the 19th century, the rise of the novel as a literary form provided a new way of reflecting the social realities of industrialization, urbanization, and class conflict. Writers like **Charles Dickens**, **Fyodor Dostoevsky**, and **Jane Austen** used their works to explore issues such as poverty, inequality, and the complexities of human relationships.

Dickens's novels, such as **Oliver Twist** and **Great Expectations**, highlighted the harsh conditions faced by the poor in Victorian England, while **Dostoevsky's works**, such as **Crime and Punishment**, grappled with questions of guilt, redemption, and moral responsibility in a rapidly changing society.

In the 20th century, literature became a powerful tool for exploring the psychological and existential crises of modernity. Writers like **James Joyce**, **Virginia Woolf**, and **Franz Kafka** pushed the boundaries of narrative form, experimenting with stream-of-consciousness techniques and fragmented structures to reflect the disorienting effects of modern life. The rise of **postcolonial literature**, with authors such as **Chinua Achebe**, **Salman Rushdie**, and **Toni Morrison**, gave voice to the experiences of colonized and marginalized peoples, challenging the dominant narratives of empire and exploring themes of identity, power, and cultural memory.

Today, literature continues to reflect and shape society, addressing contemporary issues such as climate change, migration, gender equality, and racial justice. Novels like **Margaret Atwood's The Handmaid's Tale** and **Chimamanda Ngozi Adichie's Half of a Yellow Sun** engage with themes of power, oppression, and resilience, offering readers both a reflection of current realities and a vision of potential futures.

The Role of Art, Music, and Literature in Cultural Identity and Social Movements

Creative expressions are not only reflections of society but also play a critical role in shaping **cultural identity** and fueling **social movements**. Through art, music, and literature, communities and individuals assert their identities, challenge oppression, and inspire collective action for social change.

Art and Cultural Identity

Art plays a central role in the formation and expression of **cultural identity**, serving as a visual language through which communities represent their values, beliefs, and histories. In many cases, art serves as a repository of cultural memory, preserving traditions and stories that are passed down through generations.

For indigenous communities, traditional art forms such as **pottery**, **weaving**, and **painting** are not only aesthetic expressions but also ways of preserving cultural heritage and resisting assimilation. The art of the **Navajo Nation**, for example, reflects the community's deep connection to the land and the cosmos, with intricate weaving patterns and sand paintings used in healing ceremonies and rituals.

In the context of **diaspora communities**, art becomes a way of navigating the complexities of identity and belonging. For example, the works of **Afro-Caribbean** and **African American** artists such as **Jean-Michel Basquiat** and **Kerry James Marshall** explore themes of displacement, cultural hybridity, and resistance to racism. Their art challenges dominant narratives of identity, offering new ways of seeing the experiences of Black communities in the Americas.

Art also plays a role in the formation of national identity, with governments often using art to promote a sense of unity and pride. **Public monuments**, **national museums**, and **cultural festivals** serve as platforms for celebrating the achievements and heritage of a nation, while also shaping how citizens perceive their collective identity.

Music and Social Movements

Music has long been a powerful force for social change, serving as both a form of resistance and a means of mobilizing communities for collective action. In many social movements, music plays a central role in expressing the aspirations, grievances, and demands of marginalized groups, providing a unifying soundtrack to the struggle for justice.

During the **civil rights movement** in the United States, for example, **spirituals**, **gospel songs**, and **protest anthems** became powerful tools for inspiring hope and solidarity among activists. Songs like **"We Shall Overcome"** and **"Ain't Gonna Let Nobody Turn Me Around"** were sung at marches, sit-ins, and rallies, providing a sense of unity and purpose. **Freedom songs** drew on the African American musical tradition to express the resilience and determination of those fighting for racial equality.

In the 1970s and 1980s, the rise of **punk rock** and **hip-hop** gave voice to the frustrations of young people marginalized by mainstream society. Punk bands like **The Clash** and **The Sex Pistols** used their music to critique capitalism, authoritarianism, and social inequality, while early hip-hop artists like **Grandmaster Flash** and **Public Enemy** addressed issues of poverty, police brutality, and systemic racism in their lyrics.

More recently, music has played a key role in movements such as **Black Lives Matter**, with artists like **Kendrick Lamar**, **Janelle Monáe**, and **Childish Gambino** using their music to address issues of racial injustice and police violence. Songs like Lamar's **"Alright"** and Monáe's **"Hell You Talmbout"** have become anthems of resistance, galvanizing activists and raising awareness of the struggles faced by Black communities in the United States and beyond.

Literature and Social Movements

Literature has also been a powerful tool for social change, with writers using their works to challenge injustice, inspire resistance, and envision new possibilities for the future. Throughout history, literature has given voice to the experiences of oppressed and marginalized groups, providing a platform for exploring issues of race, class, gender, and power.

During the **abolitionist movement** in the 19th century, works like **Harriet Beecher Stowe's Uncle Tom's Cabin** and **Frederick Douglass's Narrative of the Life of Frederick Douglass** helped galvanize public opinion against slavery in the United States. These works humanized the plight of enslaved Africans, exposing the brutality of the slave system and calling for its abolition.

In the 20th century, writers such as **James Baldwin**, **Toni Morrison**, and **Maya Angelou** used their literary works to explore the complexities of race, identity, and systemic oppression in America. Through novels, essays, and memoirs, these authors illuminated the struggles of African Americans and challenged the dominant narratives of race and power in the United States.

Literature has also played a key role in feminist movements, with writers like **Virginia Woolf**, **Simone de Beauvoir**, and **bell hooks** exploring the intersections of gender, power, and identity. Woolf's **A Room of One's Own**, for example, remains a seminal text in feminist literary criticism, arguing for the importance of women's creative independence and the need for female voices in literature.

In the postcolonial context, writers like **Chinua Achebe**, **Ngũgĩ wa Thiong'o**, and **Salman Rushdie** used their works to critique colonialism and its lasting impact on societies. Achebe's **Things Fall Apart**, for example, explores the tensions between indigenous African cultures and the forces of European colonialism, offering a counter-narrative to the Eurocentric depictions of Africa prevalent at the time.

Today, literature continues to be a powerful tool for social change, addressing contemporary issues such as climate change, migration, LGBTQ+ rights, and indigenous sovereignty. Through storytelling, writers invite readers to imagine new possibilities for justice, equality, and liberation.

How to Appreciate the Arts as a Way to Understand Different Perspectives and Experiences

Art, music, and literature offer more than just entertainment or aesthetic pleasure—they provide us with a way of seeing the world through the eyes of others. By engaging with creative expressions, we can gain a deeper understanding of different cultures, experiences, and perspectives, broadening our worldview and fostering empathy.

Art as a Window into Other Cultures

Appreciating art allows us to explore the cultural and historical contexts from which it emerges, providing insights into the values, beliefs, and experiences of different societies. Whether through the vibrant colors of a **Mexican mural**, the intricate patterns of **Islamic calligraphy**, or the bold abstraction of **modernist painting**, art invites us to engage with diverse ways of seeing and interpreting the world.

Visiting **museums**, **galleries**, and **public art installations** offers opportunities to encounter works from different cultures and historical periods, encouraging reflection on how art has shaped and been shaped by the social and political realities of its time. Engaging with **indigenous art**, for example, can provide insights into the spiritual and environmental values of native communities, while examining the works of **diasporic artists** can illuminate the complexities of identity, migration, and cultural hybridity.

Music as a Universal Language

Music has the unique ability to transcend language and cultural barriers, offering a universal form of expression that resonates across time and space. By exploring different musical traditions, we can gain a deeper appreciation for the diversity of human expression and the shared emotional experiences that unite us.

Listening to **classical Indian ragas**, **West African drumming**, or **Brazilian samba** allows us to experience the rhythms, melodies, and harmonies that are central to these cultural traditions. At the same time, exploring the lyrics of **folk songs**, **protest anthems**, and **hip-hop tracks** can reveal the stories, struggles, and aspirations of different communities.

Attending live performances, exploring new genres, and learning about the historical and cultural context of different musical traditions can deepen our appreciation for the richness of global music. In doing so, we can connect with the emotions and experiences of people from different parts of the world, fostering a sense of solidarity and shared humanity.

Literature as a Way of Seeing the World

Literature offers a unique opportunity to step into the minds and lives of others, allowing us to experience the world through different perspectives. By reading works from diverse authors and genres, we can gain insights into the lived experiences of people from different cultures, races, genders, and social backgrounds.

Exploring **world literature**—from the magical realism of **Gabriel García Márquez** to the existentialism of **Albert Camus**—invites us to grapple with the complexities of the human condition. Whether through fiction, poetry, or memoir, literature challenges us to question our assumptions, reflect on our values, and imagine new possibilities for the future.

By engaging with works from authors who represent marginalized communities—such as indigenous writers, LGBTQ+ authors, or writers from the Global South—we can develop a deeper understanding of the struggles and triumphs of people whose experiences may differ from our own. In doing so, literature becomes a powerful tool for cultivating empathy, expanding our worldview, and fostering cross-cultural understanding.

Conclusion

Art, music, and literature are not merely forms of entertainment or aesthetic pleasure; they are essential to understanding the world in all its complexity. These creative expressions reflect the social, political, and cultural realities of their time, offering insights into the human experience and shaping the course of history. Through art, music, and literature, individuals and communities assert their identities, challenge injustice, and inspire collective action for social change.

By appreciating and engaging with creative expressions from diverse cultures and perspectives, we can broaden our understanding of the world and deepen our connection to humanity. Whether through the bold brushstrokes of a painting, the rhythmic beat of a song, or the evocative words of a novel, the arts offer us a window into the richness of human experience, inviting us to see the world through the eyes of others and to imagine new possibilities for the future.

In a globalized world, where cultural exchange and cross-cultural understanding are more important than ever, the arts remain a powerful tool for fostering empathy, dialogue, and connection. Through art, music, and literature, we can explore the diversity of human expression and build bridges of understanding that transcend borders, languages, and differences, reminding us of our shared humanity.

Chapter 15: Future Trends and Challenges

As we move deeper into the 21st century, the world is undergoing rapid transformations, driven by technological advancements, demographic shifts, and societal changes. These emerging trends present both exciting opportunities and formidable challenges. While innovation holds the promise of addressing many of the world's most pressing issues—such as climate change, poverty, and disease—it also raises important questions about inequality, privacy, and the future of work. The complexity of these challenges demands that we not only understand current trends but also cultivate the adaptability and forward-thinking mindset necessary to thrive in an ever-changing world.

This chapter will explore the **emerging technologies, demographic shifts, and societal changes** that are shaping the future. It will also examine the **role of innovation** in addressing global challenges and discuss how individuals and societies can stay adaptable and prepared for the uncertainties of the future.

Emerging Technologies, Demographic Shifts, and Societal Changes Shaping the Future

The future is being shaped by a range of transformative forces, many of which are interlinked. These forces include advancements in technology, changes in the global population, and evolving social dynamics. Understanding these trends is key to preparing for the challenges and opportunities that lie ahead.

Emerging Technologies: Artificial Intelligence, Biotechnology, and Beyond

One of the most significant drivers of change in the 21st century is the rapid development of **emerging technologies**. Among the most transformative are **artificial intelligence (AI)**, **biotechnology**, **quantum computing**, and **renewable energy technologies**. These advancements have the potential to revolutionize industries, improve human health, and mitigate environmental problems, but they also raise ethical and practical challenges that need to be carefully managed.

Artificial Intelligence and Automation

Artificial intelligence (AI) is already transforming the way we live, work, and interact. From smart assistants like **Siri** and **Alexa** to more complex applications such as AI-powered medical diagnostics, AI is being integrated into nearly every aspect of modern life. One of the most significant impacts of AI is its ability to **automate tasks** that were previously performed by humans, leading to increased efficiency and productivity.

However, the rise of AI and **automation** also presents challenges, particularly in the labor market. Many jobs, especially those involving routine tasks in industries like manufacturing, transportation, and retail, are at risk of being automated. While automation can lead to cost savings and higher productivity, it may also result in significant **job displacement**. This raises important questions about how societies will support workers whose jobs are made obsolete by AI and automation, and how to ensure that the benefits of technological advancements are shared equitably.

At the same time, AI has the potential to unlock new opportunities in fields such as **healthcare**, **education**, and **scientific research**. AI-powered tools can analyze vast amounts of data to make more accurate diagnoses, develop personalized treatments, and even accelerate the discovery of new drugs. In education, AI could provide personalized learning experiences, helping students learn at their own pace and according to their unique needs. These possibilities demonstrate the dual nature of AI—offering both opportunities and challenges that must be carefully navigated.

Biotechnology and Genetic Engineering

Biotechnology is another area of rapid innovation that is shaping the future. Advances in **genetic engineering**, **CRISPR technology**, and **synthetic biology** are opening up new possibilities for improving human health, agriculture, and environmental sustainability. **CRISPR**, a revolutionary gene-editing technology, allows scientists to make precise changes to the DNA of living organisms, enabling the correction of genetic disorders and the enhancement of crops to be more resistant to diseases and climate change.

However, the power to edit genes also raises significant ethical concerns. The potential for **"designer babies"**, where parents could select genetic traits for their children, has sparked debates about the moral implications of altering the human genome. Moreover, the unequal access to these technologies could exacerbate existing social and economic inequalities, with only the wealthy being able to afford genetic enhancements.

In agriculture, biotechnology offers the promise of **sustainable farming** practices through the development of crops that require less water, fertilizer, and pesticides. These advancements are crucial for feeding a growing global population in the face of climate change and dwindling natural resources. However, concerns about the long-term impacts of genetically modified organisms (GMOs) on ecosystems and human health continue to fuel debates about the use of biotechnology in food production.

Quantum Computing and the Future of Technology

Quantum computing represents the next frontier in computational technology, with the potential to solve complex problems that are currently beyond the reach of classical computers. Quantum computers operate on the principles of quantum mechanics, allowing them to process vast amounts of data simultaneously. This capability could revolutionize fields such as cryptography, materials science, and drug discovery by enabling the simulation of complex molecular interactions or the breaking of encryption codes that protect sensitive data.

The development of quantum computing is still in its early stages, but its potential implications for both industry and society are profound. For example, quantum computers could help accelerate the development of new materials with unique properties, such as superconductors that operate at room temperature, leading to breakthroughs in energy efficiency. At the same time, the increased computing power of quantum machines could pose risks to **cybersecurity**, as they may be able to break traditional encryption methods, making it necessary to develop new security protocols.

Demographic Shifts: Aging Populations and Urbanization

As technology transforms the way we live and work, **demographic shifts** are reshaping the structure of societies worldwide. The two most significant demographic trends are **population aging** and **urbanization**, both of which have wide-reaching implications for global development.

Population Aging

One of the most notable demographic changes is the **aging population** in many parts of the world. Advances in healthcare and improved living standards have contributed to longer life expectancies, resulting in a growing proportion of elderly people in countries such as Japan, Germany, and the United States. According to the **United Nations**, the number of people aged 65 and older is expected to more than double by 2050, reaching over 1.5 billion.

While longer life expectancies are a positive development, they also present challenges for governments and societies. **Healthcare systems** will need to adapt to meet the needs of aging populations, particularly in managing chronic diseases such as dementia, diabetes, and heart disease. Additionally, the economic implications of aging populations—such as shrinking workforces and increased demand for pensions and social services—will require innovative solutions to maintain economic growth and social welfare.

One potential solution is the integration of **robotics** and **AI** into elder care, allowing for better monitoring and assistance for elderly individuals who require support. Technology could also play a role in enabling older adults to live independently for longer periods, reducing the strain on healthcare and social services.

Urbanization and the Growth of Megacities

Urbanization is another major demographic trend shaping the future, with more people than ever living in cities. According to the **World Bank**, by 2050, nearly 70% of the world's population is expected to live in urban areas. This shift has led to the rise of **megacities**, urban areas with populations exceeding 10 million people. Cities such as **Tokyo**, **São Paulo**, **Mumbai**, and **Lagos** are already experiencing significant population growth, and this trend is set to continue.

While urbanization can drive economic growth and innovation, it also brings challenges related to infrastructure, housing, and environmental sustainability. **Overcrowding**, **traffic congestion**, and **pollution** are common problems in megacities, putting pressure on governments to develop sustainable urban planning solutions. Additionally, urban areas are more vulnerable to the impacts of **climate change**, such as rising sea levels, extreme weather events, and heatwaves, making it essential to develop resilient and adaptable cities.

The concept of **"smart cities"** is emerging as a potential solution to the challenges of urbanization. Smart cities leverage technology and data to improve urban services, optimize resource use, and reduce environmental impact. For example, smart traffic systems can reduce congestion by adjusting traffic signals in real time, while smart energy grids can improve energy efficiency by integrating renewable energy sources. However, the widespread use of data in smart cities raises concerns about **privacy** and **surveillance**, making it crucial to strike a balance between technological innovation and protecting individual rights.

Societal Changes: Shifting Values and Global Movements

Alongside technological and demographic shifts, **societal changes** are reshaping the way people think about issues such as identity, equality, and the environment. These changes are often driven by global movements advocating for social justice, human rights, and environmental sustainability.

The Rise of Social Movements

In recent years, social movements such as **Black Lives Matter**, **Fridays for Future**, and **#MeToo** have gained global attention, highlighting issues of racial justice, gender equality, and climate change. These movements have been fueled in part by the rise of **social media**, which enables activists to organize, share information, and mobilize supporters across borders. As a result, issues that were once confined to specific regions or communities now have a global platform, encouraging collective action and raising awareness of systemic injustices.

Social movements are also driving changes in corporate behavior, as consumers increasingly demand that companies take a stand on social and environmental issues. **Corporate social responsibility (CSR)** has become a key focus for many businesses, with companies committing to ethical labor practices, reducing their carbon footprint, and promoting diversity and inclusion. The rise of **sustainable investing**—where investors prioritize companies that align with their values—further demonstrates the growing influence of social movements on the global economy.

Changing Attitudes Toward Work and Life

Another significant societal change is the evolving attitude toward work and personal fulfillment. In many parts of the world, younger generations are rejecting the traditional notions of a **career ladder** and **work-life balance**, instead prioritizing **flexibility, purpose,** and **mental well-being**. The rise of the **gig economy, remote work,** and **freelancing** reflects this shift, as more people seek alternative ways of working that offer greater autonomy and align with their personal values.

The **COVID-19 pandemic** accelerated this trend, with millions of people around the world working remotely and reevaluating their relationship with work. As companies adapt to new ways of operating, the future of work is likely to be more decentralized and flexible, with a greater emphasis on **work-life integration** and **employee well-being**. However, this shift also raises questions about **job security, income inequality,** and **access to benefits** for gig workers and freelancers, who often lack the protections afforded to traditional employees.

The Role of Innovation in Addressing Global Challenges

As the world faces a range of complex and interconnected challenges, **innovation** has the potential to provide solutions that can improve human well-being, protect the environment, and foster global prosperity. However, harnessing the power of innovation requires collaboration across sectors, investment in research and development, and a commitment to ethical and inclusive approaches.

Tackling Climate Change Through Innovation

Climate change is one of the most pressing global challenges, with far-reaching implications for ecosystems, economies, and human health. Innovation in **renewable energy**, **green technology**, and **sustainable agriculture** is essential for mitigating the impacts of climate change and transitioning to a low-carbon economy.

Renewable energy technologies such as solar, wind, and geothermal power have made significant advancements in recent years, providing cleaner and more sustainable alternatives to fossil fuels. Innovations in **energy storage**, such as **battery technology** and **hydrogen fuel cells**, are also crucial for overcoming the intermittency of renewable energy sources and ensuring a reliable supply of clean energy.

In addition to energy innovations, new technologies in **carbon capture and storage (CCS)** and **reforestation** offer promising solutions for reducing greenhouse gas emissions. **Carbon capture** technologies can capture CO_2 from industrial processes and store it underground, preventing it from entering the atmosphere. Meanwhile, large-scale reforestation efforts, supported by **drones** and **AI**, are helping to restore ecosystems and increase carbon sequestration.

Sustainable agriculture is another area where innovation is critical for addressing climate change. **Vertical farming**, **precision agriculture**, and **lab-grown meat** are among the innovations that could reduce the environmental impact of food production and increase food security in a changing climate. However, the widespread adoption of these technologies will require investment, policy support, and changes in consumer behavior.

Innovation in Healthcare and Global Health

The healthcare industry has long been a hotbed of innovation, and recent advancements in **biotechnology**, **telemedicine**, and **digital health** are poised to revolutionize the way healthcare is delivered. These innovations have the potential to improve health outcomes, reduce costs, and make healthcare more accessible to underserved populations.

One of the most promising areas of healthcare innovation is **personalized medicine**, which uses genetic information to tailor treatments to individual patients. By analyzing a patient's genetic makeup, doctors can develop more effective treatment plans, reduce the risk of adverse reactions, and improve overall outcomes. Personalized medicine is particularly important in fields such as **cancer treatment**, where genetic mutations play a key role in the progression of the disease.

Telemedicine and **digital health** platforms have also gained traction, particularly during the COVID-19 pandemic, when in-person visits to healthcare providers were limited. These technologies enable patients to consult with doctors remotely, access health information, and monitor their conditions using **wearable devices**. Telemedicine has the potential to expand access to healthcare in rural and underserved areas, where medical professionals are often in short supply.

In addition to these advancements, innovations in **vaccines** and **pandemic preparedness** will be essential for preventing future global health crises. The rapid development of **mRNA**

vaccines for COVID-19 demonstrated the potential for new vaccine technologies to be deployed quickly in response to emerging diseases. Ongoing research in **antiviral therapies**, **genomic surveillance**, and **public health infrastructure** will be critical for improving the world's ability to respond to future pandemics.

Inclusive Innovation: Ensuring Equitable Access

While innovation has the potential to address global challenges, it is essential to ensure that the benefits of innovation are distributed equitably. **Inclusive innovation** refers to the development and deployment of technologies that are accessible to all, regardless of socioeconomic status, geographic location, or demographic background.

One of the key challenges in achieving inclusive innovation is ensuring that marginalized communities have access to the resources and opportunities needed to benefit from technological advancements. This includes investing in **education and training**, particularly in fields such as **STEM** (science, technology, engineering, and mathematics), to equip individuals with the skills needed to participate in the innovation economy.

In addition to education, governments and international organizations must work to close the **digital divide**, ensuring that all individuals have access to reliable internet, affordable devices, and digital literacy programs. As more aspects of life—such as education, healthcare, and employment—move online, equitable access to digital infrastructure will be critical for reducing inequality and fostering inclusive economic growth.

Furthermore, innovation must be guided by **ethical principles** that prioritize human rights, environmental sustainability, and social justice. This includes considering the potential unintended consequences of new technologies, such as the displacement of workers, the exacerbation of inequality, or the violation of privacy. By adopting a **human-centered approach** to innovation, we can ensure that technological progress benefits all members of society.

How to Stay Adaptable and Forward-Thinking in an Ever-Changing World

In a world characterized by rapid change and uncertainty, staying adaptable and forward-thinking is essential for navigating the challenges and opportunities of the future. Whether at the individual, organizational, or societal level, cultivating **resilience**, **lifelong learning**, and **future-oriented thinking** can help us thrive in an ever-changing world.

Cultivating Resilience and Adaptability

Resilience is the ability to **bounce back** from adversity and adapt to changing circumstances. In a world of constant disruption—whether due to technological change, economic shifts, or global crises—resilience is a key trait for individuals and organizations. Developing resilience involves being open to change, embracing uncertainty, and maintaining a positive and proactive mindset in the face of challenges.

One way to build resilience is by **embracing failure** as an opportunity for growth. In both personal and professional contexts, setbacks are inevitable, but they can also provide valuable lessons. By viewing failure as part of the learning process, individuals and organizations can become more adaptable and better equipped to handle future challenges.

Lifelong Learning and Skill Development

In an era of rapid technological change, the skills needed to succeed in the workforce are constantly evolving. **Lifelong learning** is essential for staying competitive in the job market and adapting to new opportunities. This means continuously acquiring new skills, whether through formal education, online courses, or on-the-job experience.

Critical thinking, **problem-solving**, and **creativity** are among the most important skills for the future, as they enable individuals to navigate complex and unpredictable challenges. Additionally, **digital literacy** and **technological fluency** will be increasingly important as more industries are transformed by automation, AI, and digital tools.

Future-Oriented Thinking: Foresight and Scenario Planning

To stay ahead of future challenges, individuals and organizations must adopt a **forward-thinking mindset** that anticipates change and prepares for multiple possible futures. **Foresight** and **scenario planning** are tools that can help organizations and governments identify emerging trends, assess risks, and develop strategies for navigating uncertainty.

Scenario planning involves envisioning multiple potential futures based on different variables, such as technological advancements, political developments, or environmental changes. By considering a range of possible outcomes, organizations can develop flexible strategies that allow them to adapt to different scenarios as they unfold.

In addition to strategic planning, future-oriented thinking requires a **long-term perspective** that prioritizes sustainability, equity, and global well-being. This means considering the impact of current decisions on future generations and ensuring that technological and economic progress is aligned with the values of social justice and environmental stewardship.

Conclusion

The future is being shaped by a complex interplay of technological advancements, demographic shifts, and societal changes. While these emerging trends present significant challenges, they also offer exciting opportunities for innovation and progress. To navigate this rapidly changing world, individuals, organizations, and governments must remain adaptable, forward-thinking, and committed to creating a future that is both inclusive and sustainable.

By embracing **innovation**, investing in **education and skill development**, and adopting a **long-term perspective**, we can address the global challenges of the 21st century and ensure that the benefits of progress are shared by all. Whether through the development of new technologies, the promotion of social justice, or the cultivation of resilience, the choices we make today will shape the world of tomorrow.

In an ever-changing world, the key to understanding the future lies in our ability to adapt, innovate, and collaborate. By staying informed, open-minded, and proactive, we can help build a future that is not only prosperous but also just, equitable, and sustainable for generations to come.

Conclusion: Building a Holistic Understanding of the World

Throughout this book, we have journeyed through various aspects of human life, culture, science, history, and the forces that shape our ever-evolving world. We've explored the power of perspective, the lessons of history, the role of science and technology, the impact of art and culture, and the challenges and opportunities that lie ahead. This concluding chapter will recap the key concepts discussed, reflect on how readers can apply these insights in their own lives and communities, and emphasize the importance of continued learning and open-mindedness in fostering a deeper understanding of the world.

Recap of the Key Concepts Explored in the Book

This book has aimed to provide readers with a **comprehensive framework** for understanding the complexities of the world around us, breaking down knowledge into interconnected themes. Each chapter has offered a lens through which to view the world, while collectively, they form a **holistic understanding** of human experience.

The Power of Perspective

In Chapter 1, we began with the idea that **perspective** plays a central role in how we understand reality. Each person's worldview is shaped by their culture, upbringing, education, and personal experiences. Recognizing the **diversity of worldviews** allows us to see beyond our own biases and limitations. By cultivating empathy and a **global mindset**, we can better appreciate the richness of human experience and engage with the world in a more meaningful way. Understanding different perspectives fosters greater tolerance, cooperation, and mutual respect.

History as a Guide

Chapter 2 highlighted the importance of **history** as a tool for understanding the present. The events of the past have shaped the modern world, from political systems and cultural norms to technological advancements and global conflicts. By studying history, we can learn from both the successes and failures of those who came before us, avoiding the repetition of mistakes and recognizing patterns that might help us navigate the future. The past holds valuable lessons that can inform how we address present challenges, such as inequality, environmental degradation, and social injustice.

The Age of Information

In Chapter 3, we examined the **evolution of information** and its central role in shaping societies. From the printing press to the digital age, the way information is created, disseminated, and consumed has had profound effects on how people understand the world. In today's era of digital media, **information literacy** is more important than ever. Readers must be equipped to critically assess sources, identify misinformation, and navigate the vast sea of data available online. Developing these skills is crucial for making informed decisions and fostering a well-informed, engaged citizenry.

The Science of Reality

Chapter 4 focused on the importance of **science** in shaping our understanding of the physical world. The **scientific**

method—with its emphasis on evidence, experimentation, and critical thinking—has been fundamental to human progress. Science provides the tools we need to solve global challenges such as climate change, disease, and food insecurity. By embracing scientific inquiry, we can make informed choices that improve the quality of life for all people. Moreover, understanding science's role in modern life enables us to grapple with the ethical and philosophical questions posed by technological advancement.

The Economic Forces Shaping the World

In Chapter 5, we explored **economics** and the powerful role it plays in shaping societies. Economic systems like capitalism, socialism, and mixed economies affect the distribution of wealth, resources, and opportunities. Concepts such as **globalization**, **supply and demand**, and **wealth inequality** provide insights into how the world's markets function and the challenges that arise from imbalanced economic systems. Understanding these forces helps us recognize the impact of economic policies on different communities and how individuals and governments can work together to address issues like poverty, unemployment, and sustainability.

Politics and Power Dynamics

Chapter 6 delved into **politics** and the complex power dynamics that influence governance, diplomacy, and international relations. Political systems vary widely across the world, from democracies and republics to autocracies and monarchies, each with its own mechanisms for distributing power and shaping societies. The chapter also explored the importance of **civic engagement**, the role of power in shaping societies, and the way political decisions affect individuals' lives on a global scale. Readers were encouraged to understand and engage with political systems and consider the impact of their participation on shaping just and equitable societies.

Culture and Identity

In Chapter 7, we examined the role of **culture and identity** in shaping our world. Culture influences how individuals see themselves, their communities, and the broader world. **Language, religion, and traditions** form the bedrock of personal and collective identity, creating shared histories and values. The chapter also highlighted the significance of cultural exchange in an increasingly globalized world, emphasizing the need for openness to diverse perspectives and the appreciation of different cultural expressions.

The Psychology of Human Behavior

Chapter 8 introduced key concepts from **psychology** that help explain human actions, motivations, and decision-making. **Cognitive biases**, social influences, and emotional intelligence all play critical roles in shaping how individuals perceive the world and interact with others. Understanding the psychological factors that drive behavior can help individuals cultivate **empathy** and improve communication, relationships, and cooperation, both at the personal level and within larger social structures.

Technology and Its Impact on Society

In Chapter 9, we explored the transformative effects of **technology** on communication, work, and daily life. The rise of the **digital age**, artificial intelligence, and automation has reshaped entire industries and transformed how people interact with one another. The chapter also discussed the ethical dilemmas posed by new technologies, including data privacy and the implications of artificial intelligence on jobs. Recognizing these challenges allows us to responsibly harness technology for the betterment of society.

The Environment and Global Sustainability

Chapter 10 addressed the interconnectedness of **environmental systems** and the urgent need for **global sustainability**. The challenges of climate change, resource depletion, and environmental degradation are some of the most pressing issues of our time. Understanding the relationship between human activity and environmental health is critical for ensuring a sustainable future. The chapter explored ways that individuals, governments, and businesses can work together to promote **environmental conservation** and **sustainable practices**, underscoring the role of both personal responsibility and collective action.

Global Health and Wellness

In Chapter 11, we discussed the importance of **global health** and the role of public health systems in addressing issues like pandemics, malnutrition, and mental health crises. The COVID-19 pandemic underscored the interconnectedness of health on a global scale, highlighting the need for international cooperation and strong public health infrastructures. The chapter also explored how health literacy can improve individual and collective well-being, particularly in combating misinformation and promoting preventative health measures.

Religion, Spirituality, and Philosophies of Life

In Chapter 12, we explored the diverse religious and spiritual practices that have shaped human culture and ethics for millennia. Religion and spirituality offer frameworks for understanding existence, morality, and the meaning of life, while also providing a foundation for cultural identity and social cohesion. The chapter examined how religious belief systems shape worldviews and moral values, and how they intersect with philosophy, ethics, and social movements. Understanding the role of religion in society fosters greater tolerance and respect for diverse belief systems.

Conflict and Cooperation in a Globalized World

Chapter 13 focused on the causes of **global conflict**—such as war, terrorism, and geopolitical tensions—while emphasizing the importance of **diplomacy**, **international organizations**, and **peacekeeping efforts** in promoting cooperation. The chapter underscored how global cooperation is essential for addressing challenges like poverty, security, and human rights. Understanding both the drivers of conflict and the mechanisms for peace enables us to contribute to building a more peaceful and just world.

The Role of Art, Music, and Literature

In Chapter 14, we explored how **creative expressions** like art, music, and literature reflect and shape societies. These mediums provide unique insights into cultural identity, history, and social movements, allowing us to engage with different perspectives and experiences. Art has long been a powerful tool for social change, challenging injustices, inspiring activism, and offering new ways of seeing the world. Understanding and appreciating creative expressions enriches our ability to connect with others and fosters empathy.

Future Trends and Challenges

Finally, Chapter 15 looked at the **emerging trends** shaping the future, including technological advancements, demographic shifts, and societal changes. The chapter discussed how **innovation**—particularly in areas like artificial intelligence, biotechnology, and renewable energy—holds the potential to solve many global challenges. However, the chapter also emphasized the need for ethical considerations and inclusive approaches to ensure that the benefits of technological progress are shared equitably. The ability to **adapt** and stay forward-thinking will be critical in navigating the uncertainties of the future.

How Readers Can Apply These Insights to Their Own Lives and Communities

Having explored a wide range of topics, the question remains: how can readers apply these insights to their own lives and communities? The knowledge gained from this book is not just theoretical; it is meant to inspire practical action and **personal growth**.

Embracing a Global Mindset

One of the key takeaways from this book is the importance of embracing a **global mindset**. In an increasingly interconnected world, understanding and appreciating diverse perspectives is essential. Whether through travel, cultural exchange, or simply engaging with ideas from different parts of the world, cultivating a sense of global citizenship allows us to connect more deeply with others and foster mutual respect.

Readers can start by seeking out opportunities to learn about other cultures, whether through reading, participating in community events, or engaging with diverse media. Building relationships across cultural boundaries not only enriches personal experiences but also contributes to greater social cohesion and cooperation.

Engaging with Current Issues

The topics covered in this book—such as climate change, inequality, and technological advancement—are not abstract concepts; they are real-world issues that affect everyone. Readers can apply their knowledge by **staying informed** about global challenges and taking action within their communities. This might include getting involved in local environmental initiatives, advocating for social justice, or supporting policies that promote sustainability and equity.

Understanding how political systems work and participating in the democratic process is another way readers can make a difference. Whether through voting, attending town hall meetings, or engaging in activism, civic engagement is crucial for shaping the policies and decisions that affect our societies.

Promoting Critical Thinking and Information Literacy

In an age of information overload, critical thinking and **media literacy** are more important than ever. Readers can apply the lessons from this book by cultivating the ability to critically assess information, question assumptions, and seek out reliable sources. This not only helps individuals make informed decisions in their personal lives but also contributes to a more informed and engaged society.

By encouraging open dialogue and thoughtful discussion within families, schools, and communities, readers can foster a culture of curiosity and critical thinking. Sharing knowledge and challenging misinformation are essential for building a society that values truth, reason, and intellectual diversity.

Supporting Innovation and Ethical Progress

As we look to the future, innovation will be key to solving global challenges. Readers can contribute to this process by supporting **ethical innovation** in their personal and professional lives. Whether as consumers, employees, or entrepreneurs, individuals can make choices that promote sustainable practices, inclusive technologies, and equitable access to resources.

For example, supporting companies that prioritize environmental sustainability, advocating for responsible data use, and promoting the ethical application of artificial intelligence are ways in which individuals can influence the direction of technological progress. Additionally, investing in education—both personal and community-based—helps ensure that future generations have the skills and knowledge needed to navigate an increasingly complex world.

The Importance of Continued Learning and Open-Mindedness in Understanding the World

Perhaps the most important lesson from this book is that **understanding the world is an ongoing process**. The world is constantly evolving, and new information, technologies, and ideas continue to emerge. In order to truly understand the complexities of the world, we must remain open-minded, curious, and committed to **lifelong learning**.

Lifelong Learning

The pursuit of knowledge does not end with the completion of a book or course; it is a lifelong journey. Readers are encouraged to continue exploring the topics covered in this book, seeking out new sources of information and engaging with emerging ideas. This might involve attending lectures, reading books and articles, enrolling in online courses, or participating in discussion groups. The more we learn, the better equipped we are to navigate the challenges and opportunities of the world around us.

Open-Mindedness

In addition to continued learning, **open-mindedness** is essential for truly understanding the world. It is easy to become entrenched in our own beliefs and perspectives, but growth comes from the willingness to consider alternative viewpoints and engage with ideas that challenge our assumptions. Open-mindedness allows us to adapt to change, embrace diversity, and build bridges between different cultures, communities, and ways of thinking.

Fostering Curiosity and Empathy

At the heart of open-mindedness is **curiosity**—the desire to learn, explore, and understand. Cultivating curiosity not only enriches our own lives but also deepens our empathy for others. By approaching the world with a sense of wonder and a commitment to understanding, we become more compassionate and connected to the broader human experience.

Conclusion: Understanding the World as a Lifelong Endeavor

The world is a complex and dynamic place, filled with diverse cultures, histories, technologies, and ideas. To truly understand it, we must take a holistic approach—one that integrates knowledge from multiple fields and perspectives. This book has provided a framework for doing so, offering insights into the many forces that shape human life, from history and science to culture, politics, and the environment.

But understanding the world is not a destination; it is a **lifelong journey**. As new challenges and opportunities emerge, we must remain adaptable, open-minded, and committed to learning. By doing so, we can not only deepen our understanding of the world but also contribute to building a more just, equitable, and sustainable future for all.

As readers take the knowledge gained from this book and apply it to their own lives and communities, they become part of the ongoing process of shaping the world. Whether through personal action, civic engagement, or global collaboration, each of us has the power to make a difference. In the end, understanding the world is not just about knowledge; it is about connection, empathy, and the shared responsibility we have to one another and the planet.

May this book serve as a stepping stone on your journey toward a deeper understanding of the world—and may that understanding inspire you to make it a better place.

About the Author

Tom Sotis has been training consistently in various fighting methods since 1969. In addition to empty hands, weapons, and firearms skills, he is now well recognized as the leading edged weapons instructor in the world recognized for contributions to international and US federal agencies, for his specialized expertise in the use of weapons.

In the private sector, Tom trains Private Security Firms, Companies and Businesses, Firearms Groups, Combatives Groups, Martial arts organizations, High-risk groups, and Community groups.

An avid researcher on psychology and human performance, Tom became a certified Motivation Analyst licensed to administer and interpret the Reiss Motivation Profile®, the world's first scientifically validated and most accurate method of personality profiling and predicting behavior.

Tom Sotis LLC presently comprises three training companies: Truly Safer (Self-Protection), Amok Global (Use of Weapons) and Carry Safer (Defensive Shooting) as well as Performance Optimization Coaching, Motivational Profiling Analysis, and instructional videos on Tactical Knife Fighting and Unarmed Knife Defense.

An avid traveler who has visited 40 countries, presently, Tom spends most of his time writing fiction and non-fiction books.

You are invited to visit his website
www.tomsotis.com
tom@tomsotis.com

Other books by Tom Sotis

The Way of Tactics

Alexander the Great

History of Greek Warfare

Global Crime Syndicates

Bounty Hunters

Truly Safer

Sharp Strategies

Being a Good Man

The Pursuit of Meaning

Fuel for the Soul

The Echo of Our Soul

Ikigai

Unbreakable Honor

What We Believe

The Character Code

The Art of Character

Timeless Wisdom

Sacred Paths

The Science of Motivation

The Protégé

www.ingramcontent.com/pod-product-compliance
Lightning Source LLC
Chambersburg PA
CBHW060500290526
45791CB00001B/195